TO BE GODDESS
Every Woman Is A Goddess
Discover Your Domain In Which You Reign Supreme

The two most important days in your life are the day you are born and the day you find out why.
-Mark Twain

To my Grandmother and my Pop-Pop, who propelled my spiritual journey.

Introduction

Part I:

THE GLORIOUS GODDESS

Chapter 1 **To Be Goddess**

Chapter 2 **Every Woman is a Goddess**

Chapter 3 **The Triple Moon Goddess**

Part II:

THE GODDESS YOU ARE

Chapter 1 **Celebrating Your Feast Day**

Chapter 2 **Rediscovering Your Origins**

Chapter 3 **Embracing Your Purpose**

Chapter 4 **Igniting Your Element**

Chapter 5 **Setting Goals**

Chapter 6 **Owning Your Symbol**

Chapter 7 **The Domain in which you Reign Supreme**

Chapter 8 **Creating Your Epic Journey**

Chapter 9 **B.A.R.N.**

Part III:

THE GODDESS YOU WILL CONTINUE TO BE

Chapter 1 **Mirror, Mirror, on the wall, who is the Goddess of them all?**

Chapter 2 **Invoking the Goddess and Goddess Rituals**

Chapter 3 **Channeled Messages From The Goddesses**

Chapter 4 **Adoring The Everyday Goddess**

Chapter 5 **Dressing and Speaking like A Goddess**

Chapter 6 **Helping other women to see the Goddess in herself**

Chapter 7 **Moon cycles and other associations of the Goddess**

Bibliography

INTRODUCTION

*Seeing is believing, but sometimes the
most real things in the world are the
things we can't see*
-The Polar Express

In terms of spirituality, faith is required for belief. You don't want to succumb to the idea of "I'll see it when I believe it", because to believe in something (or someone) does not always require proof. Think about it for a minute; you cannot 'see' the wind, the air in which you breathe, but you can *feel* it. You see faith take place when miracles manifest, people transform and new situations arise because people believe without the need for seeing what makes it all possible.

When I was a kid, I just assumed that everyone had a gift because I was experiencing certain things that clearly were not a product of this world. I remember thinking I was adopted because I did not fit in with those around me! I just somehow knew that my mom was not actually my real mother, I saw golden sparkles in the air (later I found out they are called angel lights). I had dreams of family members and close friends of the family passing, sometimes years in advance. On one memorable occasion, I was visited by a mysterious figure in a green cloak. That story was later published a Doreen Virtue book and I found out the figure that came to me in a green cloak was the Archangel Raphael whose mission is to help heal our mind, body and spirit and to help guide those whose purpose is to be a healer.

I really felt that I was a witch. I swore that some ritual was going to take place when I turned 13 and people would say "Yay, Tia! Congratulations! We can now tell you the mystical family secrets!" Something like you'd seen on the TV show *Sabrina the Teenage Witch*...But when my 13th birthday finally rolled around, nothing happened. And so, I went on with my life and continued picking up on people's energy (of course, at that time I had no idea I was absorbing the energy of others as an Empath), knowing things about people by being claircognizant, and so forth. On one occasion, I started to get serious pains in my stomach that was not related to any explainable physical health issues (this was a development of being clairsentient, the ability to clearly feel something/event/etc). Another memorable day, I knew that something terrible had happened. I told my mom and grandmother that very night and later, in fact, something bad did happen. There was a death in our family, a cousin that I have never met. I still hadn't put together that what I was experiencing was a gift from God. I just thought it was natural and a part of everyone's life experience.

Let's fast forward to 2006, the year my grandmother died from cancer. I had a dream years earlier (actually, twice I had this dream, years apart) of her departure. I knew when she would die, but I didn't know how. Even though I knew, I tried to block that dream, to forget it. It's not easy to do so, for the visions are a great gift of God. My grandmother was slowly dying from cancer; from the time she was diagnosed, until the time she passed away were two very long years. My grandmother was very interested and understood the meaning of dreams and numbers. She knew of my intuitive gifts and she asked me if I had any dreams of her dying. I said "No" because I neither wanted to admit it nor did not want to upset my beloved grandmother. Roughly a year and a half after my grandmother's passing, my Pop-Pop also passed away. My family was terribly distraught by the passing of my grandmother and my Pop-Pop's heart was broken. My Pop-Pop went missing for a while and one day I smelled his cologne, as if he was standing next to me, and I knew that he had passed.

I had a very mystical dream after they had passed. My grandmother was in the dream and she said "Spirit has something to show you." We were in an amphitheater, sitting in the balcony, and a blue stream of sparkles come out and went serpentine into the night sky. I saw three moons; two full and one crescent. Then, I was on stage and people are clapping for me and throwing roses on stage. At age 22, that dream was my initiation, the ritual I was looking for when I was 13. My grandmother and Pop-Pop were very instrumental in raising me and once they passed, they became instrumental in my spiritual journey as well. The result of the dream and a, roughly, two- year healing period lead to the creation of The Violet Sanctuary Spa, LLC in 2010 and this book before you; it was my Divine Inspiration coordinated by my wonderful grandparents.

My prayer is that we all acknowledge our spiritual gifts, help those who want to be helped, and treasure the people in our lives. This book is a tool that can be used over and over again to aid you in your spiritual journey. This book is comprised of my experiences, channeled messages from the Goddess, and studies of what makes a Goddess. *Every* woman is a Goddess. We just need to *remember* who we are. It is my main goal that you tap into your ultimate source of power as a Goddess; increasing your self-confidence, spiritual awareness, spiritual gifts, and so much more!

This book is not a "how to" book because you are already a powerful Goddess. This book will actually help you tweak your world or, as I like to call it "realm", so that you *own* it and the people around you will know it through your powerful presence (although they might not be able to explain it). As for the Gentlemen reading this book, no worries; just replace *Goddess* with *God* and most the information still applies. While reading this book, you will experience a lot of firm, powerful, energy as well as gentle energy. This book is meant to be informal like a conversation between old friends and if you believe in past lives like me, then we are in fact old friends!

This book has three parts. Part I is to introduce you to the concept of To Be Goddess and the goddesses I worked with during the creation of this book. Part II is all about you owning your goddess status. Part III is applications and other sacred information about the goddess and living the goddess life. In short, this is an interactive book with a myriad of meditations, illustrations, thought provoking questions, and so much more.

May you enjoy the journey of diving into your ultimate goddess form and may you enjoy meeting and working with the goddesses!

Goddess Blessings,

Tia Johnson

Internationally known, Tia Johnson has several of her angel stories published in spiritual books. In addition, Tia is a Gateway Dreaming™ Coach, certified by Denise Linn, a Certified Reiki Practitioner, an ANGEL THERAPRY PRACTITIONER®, certified by Doreen Virtue, PhD, and a Hibiscus Moon

Certified Crystal Healer. Listen to her radio show, which currently airs weekly online at www.blogtalkradio.com/thevioletsanctuaryspa. To find out more about Tia and her work, visit her website at www.violetsanctuaryspa.com.

PART I

The Glorious Goddess

CHAPTER I
TO BE GODDESS

God, protect me; Goddess, nurture me.
-Tia Johnson

I believe that every woman is a goddess, **many just need to remember their connection to Spirit. Here's what I have realized through my personal experience and spiritual journey**:

- Some women just have to remember who they are, a glorious goddess
- Little girls are goddesses as well, but they are at a stage of the very young maiden
- Some women have worries about being called divine, being overpowering, or standing out
- Some women are well into their goddess power and know exactly what they want
- Every woman has her niche
- We are all connected

Over the years, I have learned that no matter what others might believe or say, there is, for many, an undeniable need and want to pursue something magical, something greater than our selves; and in most cases, we know exactly or partly what it is. We just *feel* like there is something more, like we are meant to do more and are completely capable of it. Often, we may call these feeling our "gut instincts", but it is actually our gifts, our intuition, the goddess (among other divine beings) guiding and nurturing us to remember who we are and what our mission is on this planet.

What does "To Be Goddess" really mean and how does it apply to you? Let's break down the phrase to the title of my book to see. The phrase "to be" is like saying you have been chosen, it is similar to saying "I am". For instance, *I am* Divine. We can further break down the phrase "to be" to "he is", "she is", "they are", and so forth; but for this book, we will focus on "I am" or "I am chosen". Now let's put it in a meaningful affirmation: "I know that I AM chosen to be a glorious goddess" or "I am a glorious goddess". How do you know you are chosen? Well, you're a female with great intuition that has been given to you by Spirit. That's how. So, step up and claim your goddess birth rite and live the goddess life!

Now, let's direct our attention to the second half of the title phrase, Goddess. Several synonyms for the word goddess are:

- Deity
- Supernatural or Divine being
- Divinity
- Spirit

The Goddess, along with the God, is the Great Spirit, the great healer, the great lover, and the great weaver of life. To be Goddess is to be connected to Spirit and the gifts Spirit has to offer. The Goddess isn't just one divine female with just a few skill sets. She is a multitude of women with a multitude of gifts, each one connected to form the oneness. The Goddess is the Egyptian goddess Isis, the Norse goddess Freyja, and the Celtic goddess Bridgit and so on. The Goddess is also, our mother, our sister, our niece, our daughter and so forth. The goddesses represent healing, love, sex, compassion, death and rebirth, sacred teachings, mysteries, strength, wisdom, destruction and rebuilding. So, if you have an annoying aunt, she may be the goddess of chaos!

To Be Goddess will mean that you will be one and all at the same time…one divine woman, but with many accomplishments, tasks, roles and responsibilities. In the words of Dr. Wayne Dyer, "we are spiritual beings having a human experience". Let's think about the different roles women have each day and we will quickly see just how supernatural we are:

- The mother
- The wife
- The girlfriend
- The best friend
- The worker
- The shopper

- The cook
- The cleaner
- The nurturer
- The student
- The teacher
- The sexy woman
- The priestess
- The leader
- The seducer
- The witch
- The one who schedules the doctors' appointments
- The one who balances the banks accounts
- The daughter/ daughter in law
- And the list goes on…

What I stated above applies to women, in one way or another, all over the world and each day we put our best foot forward knowing that we have done our job. But, at times, we would like to receive some appreciation! There's a fine line, however, because the appreciation we desire could be a result of constantly going above and beyond while refusing to delegate or being a "control freak" without giving people a chance to do things their way. We feel like we have to do everything and we often develop a "martyr" complex; do things to a point where we become burnt out. Sometimes we also expect people to do things for us without asking for help, and then complain about not being appreciated. This is *not* the way "To Be Goddess", it is playing the victim which is never connected to Spirit.

The supposed appreciation we want, because we do so much, can cause friction within the family, between friends, and then we look disingenuous for doing things we did not want to do and for expecting something in return. The key here is balance. While goddesses are known to accomplish many tasks, they also recruited other divine beings or created tools to help them if it was required. Did they lose their divine status? No, not at all! It made them stronger. That's right; seeking help and not doing it all alone makes you stronger.

Many goddesses send their symbols to help you along your path. They send symbols, such as an animal, because you may be, at the time, more receptive to seeing the goddess' animal as a sign of confirmation in regards to an issue that has been on your mind. It's about connection and what is most comfortable to you. So, if you're a bit nervous about seeing the very sexy Nordic goddess Freyja, then she may give you a vision of a lion, or if feeling the intensity of Celtic goddess Brigit's illumination is a bit much, then she may give you a vision of a bright candle. All these symbols or messages are sent to communicate with you, guide you and help you, because going it alone is not "To Be Goddess."

Below, are several goddesses and a few of their symbols. You will understand the meanings when you connect with the goddesses for the meaning will vary for each person.

GODDESS	SYMBOL/ANIMAL
ISIS, Egyptian moon goddess of divine magic, healing, and balance life	FULL MOON, ANKH, CIRCULAR DISK WITH HORNS HEADDRESS, COBRA, SPARROWHAWK, CRAB
FREYJA, Norse goddess of war, love, sex and sensuality	AURORA BOREALIS (THE NORTHERN LIGHTS), SWORD, SPINNING WHEEL, THE DAY FRIDAY, CATS, SPARROWS, HORSES, FALCONS
QUAN YIN, Chinese goddess of compassion and fertility; also known as 'she who hears all prayers'	WHITE LOTUS, THE NUMBER 33, WILLIOW BRANCHES, ROSARY IN HAND
BRIGIT, Irish/Celtic triple moon goddess, goddess of the Sacred Flame, and protector; also known as Saint Brigid	FIRE, HEARTH, LIGHT, CANDLE, SUNRISE, COW, ENTWINED SNAKES, OWLS, THE TRIPLE MOON

GODDESS	SYMBOL/ANIMAL
ATHENA, Grecian goddess of wisdom, arts and crafts; warrior goddess	GOLDEN SHIELD AND HELMET, NUMBER 7, BLACK PIGEON, OLIVE TREE, OWL
DANA, Irish/Celtic goddess of manifestations and alchemy; mother goddess of Tuatha Dé Dananns; also known as High- Priestess of Divine magic	WATER, WELLS, FISH, BLACK CAULDRON FILLED WITH WATER; VISITATIONS FROM ELEMENTALS SINCE SHE'S THE MOTHER OF ELEMENTALS, SUCH AS LEPRECHAUNS
KALI, Hindu goddess of cycles, transformation, death, birth, and rebirth; overcoming procrastination	BLACK, BRIGHT RED, BRIGHT RED TOUNGE, DARK (NEW) MOON, I PERSONALLY TEND TO HEAR DRUMS BEATING
LILITH, Sumerian/Hebrew goddess of the wind, great strength and sexuality	OWL, SNAKE, DARK (NEW) MOON
CERRIDWEN, Welsh dark moon goddess of the cauldron, brewer of divine wisdom, inspiration, and transformation; triple moon goddess, crone aspect	CAULDRON, THE WHITE SOW, TRIPLE MOON, DARK (NEW) MOON

GODDESS	SYMBOL/ANIMAL
LAKSHMI, Hindu moon goddess of abundance	ELEPHANT, LOTUS, WATER, GOLDEN COINS
APHRODITE, Grecian goddess of beauty, love, and pleasure	OCEAN, SEASHELL, GOLDEN APPLES, MIRROR, TRIANGEL, DOLPHIN, DOVE, SWAN
PELE, Volcanic Hawaiian goddess of fire, transformation, seduction, passion, and heart's true desire	FIRE, WHITE DOG, VOLCANO
IX CHEL, Mayan moon goddess of healing, life cycles, mother goddess of Mayan deities; also known as 'Lady Rainbow'	JAGUAR, RAINBOW, WHITE, WATER

Since you are indeed a glorious goddess, you are a magical woman! You create realities and manifest your needs and wants. How do you know you're magical? Let's, read below:

- ഔ You are reading this book for one. Spirit has guided you here to learn about your goddess nature
- ഔ Certain things just feel natural to you like working with crystals, herbs, and the elements
- ഔ You work with magical beings like fairies, goddesses, angels, and elements
- ഔ You visit places and remember things without explanation, have flashbacks of a past life, or felt like you have been there before.

My definition of the word goddess is a powerful, magical woman who is in sync with the energies around her. "To Be Goddess" applies to you because you simply are a goddess. Even when you feel like you're not, you still are. "To Be Goddess" does not always mean an easy path; there are goddesses who have experienced suffering. For example, Isis had to search the Earth for her husband's, Osiris, body parts after his brother killed and dismembered him.

To Be Goddess Sacred Prayer

Goddess, help me to remember who I am

And what it is I'm meant to do.

Grant me wisdom, clairvoyance, compassion, strength, and the ability to understand what needs to be done without further ado.

Illuminate my path to show me the way.

Show me how to use my gifts by visiting me in my dreams every night and every day.

To Be Goddess is the path.

To Be Goddess is who I AM.

To Be Goddess is a way of life for me.

I bathe in the elements and reconnect with all that is. I radiate beauty and light for all eternity.

CHAPTER 2
EVERY WOMAN IS A GODDESS

You already know her. It is she who moves you in your dance.
She is the music of your life. Do you need to ask her name?
-The Goddess Path

Don't you dare, not even for a moment, think you're not gifted enough, pretty enough, shapely enough, sporty enough or, because you have a disability, that you cannot be a goddess. When you are feeling low with your self esteem, music is a great way to uplift your spirits. Music can deliver a powerful message with its lyrics and melody; which is why I love P!nk's song F**kin Perfect, because she tells a story about acceptance and obstacles.

If you ever had a doubt about being a goddess; then, really listen to her song.
It's a powerful message with a melody. Every woman is a goddess, no exceptions!

The key to improving your self worth is not to ignore the proverbial elephant in the room. I want you to address your feelings about why you believe you cannot be a goddess and then we are going to blast away those thoughts with help from Kali, the very powerful Hindu goddess of change and cycles. Not only will she help you to overcome obstacles that go against your highest good, she will help you to defy procrastination so that you will be on the fast track of your spiritual journey.

Sometimes, we just need someone to help us to see the goddess within and there is nothing wrong with being willing to receive help! Remember to keep an open mind and the possibilities are endless, but we have to make the first step of believing that we can change and knowing that help is available. Below, I have created a list of some popular issues and how Kali can help us to overcome those issues.

ISSUE	THOUGHT PROCESS	BLAST AWAY
I HAVE ADDICTIONS	BY MY WILL AND HELP FROM SPIRIT I WILL OVERCOME ADDICTIONS	GODDESS KALI, I'M READY TO HAVE MY WORLD REBUILT
I'M NOT PRETTY	I SET MY OWN STANDARDS OF WHAT IS PRETTY	GODDESS KALI, I'M PREPARED TO CREATE A NEW OUTLOOK ABOUT MYSELF
I'M OVERWEIGHT	I EMBRACE MYSELF FIRST THROUGH LOVE AND LEAD A HEALTHY LIFE	GODDESS KALI, I'M READY TO REMOVE THE OBSTACLE OF WEIGHT FROM MY PATH
I HAVE NO TALENT	I JUST HAVE UNTAPPED ABILITIES WAITING TO BE DISCOVERED	GODDESS KALI, I'M WILLING TO GO INTO THE UNKNOWN TO DISCOVER MY TALENTS
I DON'T KNOW WHERE TO BEGIN	MAY THE GODDESS GIVE ME CLEAR DIRECTION	GODDESS KALI, I'M READY TO BEGIN A NEW CYCLE
I'M AFRAID	MAY THE GODDESS GRANT ME THE STRENGHT TO BE COURAGEOUS AND HAVE FAITH	GODDESS KALI, I'M WILLING TO CHANGE MY ATTITUDE
I'M NOT STRONG	WITH EACH STEP I TAKE TOWARDS LIVING MY PURPOSE, I BECOME STRONGER	GODDESS KALI, TEACH ME TO BE AS STRONG AS YOU
I HAVE DISABILITIES	WHAT MAY HINDER ME PHYSICALLY, DOES NOT HINDER MY SPIRIT FOR MY SPIRIT SOARS	GODDESS KALI, SHOW ME HOW TO RELEASE MY SPIRIT TO NEW HEIGHTS
I'M NOT SMART	I HAVE JUST ENOUGH KNOWLEDGE TO KNOW WHAT I NEED TO DO OR WHO TO CONTACT FOR HELP	GODDESS KALI, SHOW ME HOW TO DO AWAY WITH ANY OBSTACLES I FACE THAT CHALLENGES MY ABILITES

ISSUE	THOUGHT PROCESS	BLAST AWAY
I DON'T DESERVE/HAVEN'T EARNT THE RIGHT	IT'S MY LIFE AND I DESERVE ALL THE GREATNESS THERE IS TO OFFER	GODDESS KALI, GRANT ME THE VISION AND STRENGHT TO SEE MYSELF AS A GOOD DESERVING PERSON OF GREAT THINGS
I DON'T UNDERSTAND MY 'SPIRITUAL JOURNEY'	FAITH AND TRUST ARE BY MY SIDE. WHAT I DON'T UNDERSTAND NOW WILL BE UNDERSTOOD WITHIN DIVINE TIMING	GODDESS KALI, SHOW ME HOW TO BE A TRAILBLAZER BY KEEPING THE FAITH AND BEING OPEN TO RECEIVING MORE MESSAGES FROM SPIRIT
I DON'T HAVE THE MONEY, TIME, OR OTHER RESOURCES	LIMITED THINKING IS NOT ACCEPTED. AS I PROCEED, THE UNIVERSE WILL GRANT ME TIME, MONEY, AND OTHER RESOURCES	GODDESS KALI, GRANT ME THE ABILITY TO ACHIEVE MY GOALS WITHOUT LIMITATION
I DON'T KNOW HOW TO EXPRESS MYSELF	I WILL BEGIN TO EXPRESS MYSELF THROUGH THE CLOTHES I WEAR, THE HAIR STYLES I CHOOSE, AND SO FORTH	GODDESS KALI, TEACH ME TO DANCE THE DANCE OF LIFE WITH PASSION AND EXPRESSION AS YOU DO

Goddess Spiral Dance Decree

Goddess Kali, I come to you open arms, ready to dance.

I'm ready to dance the dance of life, to embrace the untamed goddess.

I will dance alongside the transformative element of fire, become powerful and take my stance.

My body will move in serpentine and spiral motions as I stomp my feet and declare to the Universe that I am one with all that is.

Goddess Kali, I embrace the dark moon, the end and the beginning of cycles.

Let no obstacles deter me from my goals.

I am power, I am one, I am grateful.

Now is the time. I hear the Divine whisper. I am prepared for I am in goddess mode.

CHAPTER 3
THE TRIPLE MOON GODDESS

Remember there are only two things without
Limits—femininity, and the means to explore it.
From the movie La Femme Nikita

The three phases of a woman, the maiden; the mother; and the crone, are what make up the triple moon goddess. Do you have to be a biological mother to experience that phase or the typical pictures we see of an old haggardly looking woman to experience the crone phase? Of course not! These are merely stages, all of which is a rite of passage celebrating you!

As a maiden:
- You are innocent
- You are younger/blossoming from girl to woman
- You are new to something/ at the beginning of a cycle/learning
- You are playful and romantic
- You see the world in its purity
- You are passionate and sensual, as an older maiden

As a mother:
- You could be a business owner in which your 'baby' is your business that you have to nurture in order for it to grow
- You could actually be a mother
- You are at the mid-point of a cycle
- You are nurturing/ protecting
- You are middle aged/ mature
- You are at the peak of your power/in control of your sexuality

As a crone:
- You are wiser/ the counselor/teacher
- You see the shadow and light side of the world
- You are at the end of a cycle
- You are older
- You are a grandmother

I like to think of the triple moon as the daughter, mother, and grandmother. You can associate with something similar, like princess, queen, and goddess. The triple moon also represents cycles. So, think about where you are in your life and how that corresponds to the triple moon goddess. Don't think age-wise per se; instead, imagine your life is a huge panoramic picture that you can just step back and look at as a whole. Now, think, is there and area in your life that is new, such as a relationship or job? Next, think about something you were involved in and helped in its growth like a purchasing a home. Then, think of something that has made you wiser, such as leaving a dead end relationship. These types of circumstances (phases) represent the triple moon goddess.

Another way to look at it is that the triple moon goddess also represents the cycle of birth, life, and death (and rebirth). That translation can be literal or figurative. For example, the literal translation would be the cycle of our lives: we are born, we live, we die, and we are reborn again. However, the figurative translation would be the cycles of the moon. First, the waxing moon, the time when the moon phase is increasing from new moon to full moon, represents the maiden aspect of our lives. Second, the full moon, the time when we can see the full moon clearly, represents the mother aspect of our lives. Third, the waning moon, the time when the moon phase is decreasing from full moon to new moon, represents the crone aspect of our lives. The new moon, also known as the dark moon, is the time when we cannot see the moon represents the time of death and soon to be rebirth.

Hence, you are ever changing. Think about it for a moment. Each year is another year you get to start fresh. Think about the months of the year from the triple moon goddess perspective.
- Spring: March 20-June 20 is the time of the young maiden
- Summer: June 21- September 21 is the time of the older maiden
- Autumn: September 22-December 20 is the time of the mother

- Winter: December 21- March 19: time of the crone, but also the time of death leading to rebirth
- And the cycle begins again the following year.

You can connect with the following goddess per particular phase you are experiencing in your life. Note that some goddesses represent more than one aspect of the triple moon; just like the goddess, you will be in multiple phases throughout your life.

THE MAIDEN	THE MOTHER	THE CRONE
APHRODITE	BRIGIT	BRIGIT
ATHENA	DANA	CERRIDWEN
BRIGIT	IX CHEL	KALI
FREYJA	KUAN YIN	PELE
LILITH	LAKSHMI	
	PELE	
	ISIS	

Here is a meditation to help you know where you are in your triple moon goddess cycle:
Get a pen and a sheet of paper.
Take a deep breath and center by asking Spirit to cleanse your area.
If possible, drink some water.

Now, mentally ask the maiden goddesses to show you what you need to know from this area in your life by saying, 'Aphrodite, Athena, Brigit, Freyja, and Lilith, the darling maiden goddesses, what do you want me to know?'

Take your time and don't worry if you think you will mistake one goddess for another; remember that each goddess has a vibration and symbols that will help you to identify them.

Next, mentally ask the mother goddesses the same question, 'Brigit, Dana, Ix Chel, Kuan Yin, Lakshmi, Pele, and Isis, the nurturing mother goddesses, what do you want me to know?'
Again, take your time while receiving the messages.

Last, mentally ask the crone goddesses the question, Brigit, Cerridwen, Kali, and Pele, the very wise crone goddesses, what do you want me to know?'

Be patient and remember to write everything down that comes to mind.

PART II

The Goddess You Are

CHAPTER 1
CELEBRATING YOUR FEAST DAY

The more you praise and celebrate your life, the more there is in life to celebrate.
–Oprah Winfrey

The term feast day is a day, especially a church holiday, for feasting and rejoicing. Well, in addition, I consider birthdays to be a holiday worthy of such festivities, in which feasting, celebrating, and honoring take place. Think about all the various holidays and feast days. Saints have a feast day. And, what about holidays like December 25 when we celebrate Christmas or July 4th to honor the birth of a nation. All of these great days are significant and celebrated when we come together to honor the meaning of them. So, why not honor your birthday? No, it's not just another day. It's a big deal because you are significant and there is no one quite like you in the universe! You are a divine being and your birthday should be considered a holiday. Therefore, when you celebrate your birthday, you are celebrating and honoring you! Here are a few things to consider for your feast day:

- Do you celebrate your birthday for a day/weekend?
- Do you want your birthday to be a main event, like going to a club or taking a trip, or something more intimate, like a small dinner party or just a table for two?
- Who would you invite to celebrate your birthday?
- Where would you celebrate your birthday?
- What does your birthday mean to you?
- Why not celebrate your birthday? In other words, what's holding you back?
- When was the last time you truly enjoyed celebrating your birthday?

Your birthday is a special time to celebrate the gift of 'you' to the world.
-Author Unknown

Now think, if you had no limits whatsoever, what would the ideal birthday be for you? I also want you to think about a ritual that you (or you and your husband/wife/bestfriend/etc) will do for your birthday. For example, a lady I used to work with always wears a dress on her birthday and her birthday is in October! My best friend does not work on her birthday because she considers it a holiday. I sing the song 'it's my party and I cry if I want to…' and on my birthday cake I always get my name written on it and I eat my name! These acts or traditions are what make a birthday significant and give it extra energy, making the day very important instead of some random day your mom was in pain, years ago, just to bring some kid to the planet! If you don't have a ritual or don't know where to begin, then see below for a few suggestions:

- Figure out what day your birthday is on so that you can plan better, say for a birthday weekend if it falls on a Friday or Saturday
- Give the people who you want to share your Feast Day/Holiday with at least a two weeks' notice so that they can give you their full attention when they arrive at your gathering instead of having mixed feelings about being able to attend because of late notification
- Think about what you love to do and make that the center of your Feast Day/Holiday. So, if you love to dance, start looking for that ultimate dancing dress ASAP and plan to go to a place (or host your party) where the music is hip and you can shake it!
- Do you have a signature drink, such as a margarita on the rocks, a comso, vodka and cranberry, or just tequila shots?! Get a distinctive glass and drink from it on your Feast Day.
- Have a favorite song? Play it in the morning to get you pumped up!
- Take a trip! You can save your money (you always have a year to do so!) and go to where ever your heart desires!
- Have a fave dish, dessert or otherwise? Make sure you tell your friends so they can make or buy it for you.
- If you can, take the day off! It is a holiday, afterall.
- Be bold! Do something you wouldn't normally do like dye your hair a different color. Turning a milestone age…get a tattoo! Or, at least the sticker tattoo! lol
- Have a great dinner! Invite a few close people to your house or make dinner reservations at a restaurant.
- Blog about your birthday and what it means to you each year.
- Of course, you can take the ultimate vacation by sleeping until noon, watch all the shows you dvr'd and have your spouse order pizza!

My experiences in regards to celebrating birthdays is that as a kid, it's definitely about having tons of friends, loads of gifts, and a really cool birthday cake. As a young adult, it was all about partying with all who would come out to celebrate my birthday. As an adult, it is about celebrating it with people whom I care about the most in a more relaxed setting, like a dinner at a restaurant or a trip to a particular destination.

Stated below are a few goddesses' feast days and rituals associated with the goddesses.
- The birthday of Isis is celebrated on July 17th. Gatherings and various rituals are held near bodies of water.
- The vow Kuan Yin committed to in order to heal all of humanity is celebrated on July 12th. Special songs are sung in honor of Kuan Yin.
- The feast day of Brigit is celebrated on February 2nd, which is also known as Imbolc, a fire festival marking a time where the Sun begins to shine stronger. Rituals such as sharing bread with a fellow neighbor are done in order to bring the goddess' good will to the home.
- The ancient Roman Festival of Love took place on February 14-21th in honor of Aphrodite. We celebrate February 14 by giving chocolates or other gifts to our loved ones.

With the first light of sun, bless you. When the day is done, bless you. In your smile and in your tears, bless you. Through each day of all your years, bless you.
-An Irish Birthday Blessing

CHAPTER 2
REDISCOVERING YOUR ORIGINS

When sleeping women wake, mountains move.
-Chinese Proverb

Each Goddess has a point of origin. For example, Aphrodite the Goddess of love, beauty, and sex, is Grecian; however, she is from 'sea foam', as her name implies. In a way, we can associate our origins with the sea as well. For example, we are mostly made up of water, while in the womb we are surrounded by water, and we need water to survive. What I would like for you to do is ask about the day you were born and then think about the day you 'knowing' began your spiritual journey. These are two different 'births" that will trigger an awaking process because you will be tapping into the depths of the physical you as well as the spiritual you. Thus, remembering who you truly are and what you are meant to do on this beautiful planet!

So, let's begin by asking a few questions:
- How were you born, meaning C-section, natural birth, water birth, etc?
- Where were you born?
- Who was present at your birth?
- What condition were you in at birth? For example, I was born two weeks late, upside down with the umbilical cord wrapped around my neck while my brother was born premature.
- When were you born, day or night?

If you were adopted and don't have access to finding out the information above, you can ask the following questions:
- What's my earliest memory of my family?
- How were they able to choose me?
- Who was involved in the process of the adoption? Names are important because there

> may be a person who has an angel or goddess name who was instrumental in the process
>
> ෩ When did my parents decide that it was time to adopt?

After you receive the answers, look for a theme. For example, if you were born at night are you more inclined to hang out with friends all night long and do you find yourself doing most of your meditation/ritual work at night? If you were born during the summer months, then do you favor the heat more so than the cold? Of course, just because you were born during one of the summer months does not mean that you don't like the cold. Instead it's more of a thought process. This is all part of your make up to better define who you are.

What if your mother had a complicated birth? This could mean that you have a warrior spirit, determined to overcome odds. This is the case for my brother. Our mother was on bed rest, he was born prematurely, and he spent thirty-days in intensive care. But, my brother has a strong will. He will not give up on his friends when they have doubts about themselves and he's always determined to succeed.

For those who were adopted, think about that special day. Was the day you were adopted sunny, rainy, etc? Now, when you travel on such days is it special to you? Really think about the early stages of that transition from where you were to being with your new family.

By rediscovering your origins, you will begin to gain an idea of where you are going in life. For example, when I was a child, around the age of five, I felt like I was adopted. I also remember feeling like I was from a special galaxy where things where just different. I had dreams about sparkly crystals prior to gaining any formal knowledge about crystals. I even had a friend in grade school named Krystal who told me that she had special powers. Not to mention that just about every year I was a witch for Halloween, with the exception of one time when I was a My Little Pony.

Looking back at those memories helped me to realize that I am truly a spiritual being having a human experience. We all are! It also helped me to realize that I have had past lives and understand why I like certain things and why I cannot tolerate other things, such as watching movies about witched being burnt at the stake.

To help you rediscover your origins, so you can discover and fine tune your purpose, you can do the following meditation:

A Meditation to Rediscover Your Origins

- If possible have meditation music with the sound of water playing
- Have a paper and a pen ready so that you can write about your experiences
- Take several deep slow breaths
- As you are taking your deep breaths, begin to close your eyes
- Ask Archangel Michael to clear your space and protect your space throughout your meditation
- Imagine yourself gently walking towards a small pond in an enchanted forest
- Look into the sparkly pond
- As you gaze into the pond, you notice the water begins to ripple and imagines appear
- Ask the pond to reveal to you what you need to know about your origins
- Ask the pond to reveal to you what you want to know
- Make time to observe the visions you see for there is no need to rush
- Thank the pond for these revelations and give it blessings
- Turn around, walk away from the pond ensuring it that you will return soon
- Open your eyes and welcome back!

CHAPTER 3
EMBRACING YOUR PURPOSE

What is success? I think it is a mixture of having a flair for the thing that you are doing; knowing that it is not enough, that you have got to have hard work and a certain sense of purpose.
-Margaret Thatcher

Each goddess has a purpose or purposes. Goddesses will come to us during various times in our lives to help us with our purposes because it's in alignment with theirs. And it is through that connection that we will be successful in fulfilling our purpose, whether it's to be a holistic healer or a non-fiction writer! Chances are, you have an idea, but you just have to tweak your journey a bit so you can capitalize on that purpose or purposes. And, some of you are thinking ...umm no, Tia, I haven't the slightest idea. Well, let's help you with the following questions.

1. What are you capable of doing well?
2. Do people compliment you on being a good listener, lover, friend, dresser, etc?
3. Are you creative or critical?

I ask this because, from my experiences, here's what they can equate to as far as life purposes are concerned:

1. A good listener=great objective advice=great blogger/columnist/start online radio show
2. A good dresser=someone who is always up-to-date=start youtube video/website providing fashion tips
3. A great lover=someone who is young at mind and adventurous= dating/sex adviser on social media/website
4. Great at influencing people=great motivator=great life coach/ get people pumped to do their life's work
5. Talk with your hands/hands on person= reiki/demonstrator
6. A very patient person= teacher
7. A traveler= start a business taking people to spiritual sites

8. Love to read= start a spiritual book club, write a book

Once you discover what your purpose is, you will begin to transform into the person you need to be in order to fulfill your purpose! It will all feel natural to you mainly because you will not notice some of the changes, but the people around you definitely will!

> *And so she reached the place where she could have stepped into the light...But Miao Shan remembered all those who still suffered...And so the girl made a vow: to remain on earth until every living thing was holy...And thus was the girl transfigured...She became the compassionate Kuan-Yin...answering every prayer addressed to her.*
> -The Goddess Path

If you are capable of doing something well, then do your research to see what opportunities are available and never stop learning!

You know when you're fulfilling your purpose because more things will begin to align. For example, you came to the conclusion that your life purpose involves cooking. So, you announce to the Universe that you are ready, willing, and able to take on this purpose of by becoming a master chef. The first thing you notice is a television commercial selling a new and improved pots and pans set. Next, your friend reminds you that it's restaurant week and plans should be made to make reservations at one of the participating restaurants. After that, your mom buys a knife set. While on the bus, the person sitting next to you makes 'small talk' about going back to school. And, finally you realize that it's time to go to culinary school. But how do you go about applying? Where do you apply? Who will help you? When should you apply? Well let's answer these questions! Just think about the questions and take your time answering each one.

How to go about applying:

Make sure you do your homework. Make sure you choose the right school, apply for financial aid, etc. Also, make arrangements job wise. If you are planning to quit your 'day job' make sure you saved the money and other aspects. Now, your turn, fill in the blank and/or say it out loud: 'I will go about applying for _____ by _____ '.

Where to apply:
Think of the city and state in which you want apply. Be sure to consider the entire city as you will want to have a life outside school as well. Do you want to stay close to home? Maybe close to a beach? Or, maybe you'll go where you'll receive the most financial aid. Whatever you do, you want to make sure that you make the most informed decision because you will be taking responsibility. Therefore, you become more likely to acknowledge when something is not working and make adjustments. Now, your turn, fill in the blank and/or say out loud: 'Where I apply depends on _____'.

What will it take for me to complete this task?
In order to complete _____, I will have to work during the (weekend, later at night, during lunch). For example, to complete this book, I wrote during my lunch break, at night after dinner, on the weekends, and sometimes while I was on the bus or train!
I'm willing to make more time to do this, which could mean less time (hanging out with the girls, guys).

Who will be instrumental in helping me?
Your support system means everything! I'm so thankful for my brothers for helping me by doing things like going to the Post Office and for my mom for letting me commandeer her living room with my three piles of stacked books and countless papers, oracle card decks and crystals, candles and two laptops! So, think about who will be helping you along your process and how that will affect them. I know that I will need the help of_____ in order to complete _____.

The dreaded 'why': Don't concern yourself with the 'whys' of the matter because why should I bother to do this will lead to I should've, could've and so forth. Just know that your intuition is never wrong. You have a purpose and it's important!

When to proceed:
There's no time like the present! Don't let 'the small stuff' get in the way like time and space. Think, I will proceed today by _____. Make the first step and watch your spiritual path illuminate, guiding you

to your next step!

Dream Board:

Dream boards work wonders! I believe dream boards work because when we constantly see images of what it is we desire, in addition to our positive reinforcement, we believe in it more because every day we 'see' it as something that we can obtain. Also, it's a really cool arts and crafts project that allows you to direct *your* energy into something awesome from conception of the idea to fruition.

Tips on creating a dream board:

- Be as creative as you like, there are no limits here
- You can use a huge construction board paper or a small one it's up to you
- Place a really awesome picture of you in the middle of the board
- Decorate, write affirmations, etc
- Remember this board is about you, so don't feel like you're being selfish
- Place the board in a place for 'your eyes only' because you don't want others negative energy filtering over into your board
- You can share your board with like minded supportive people (I made my first dream board with my brother!)
- You can make as many dream boards as you like, but make sure to give them all attention by looking over them throughout the day.
- Feel everything you placed on that board as the ultimate truth! You need to believe in yourself and what you want to create in your life!

CHAPTER 4
IGNITING YOUR ELEMENT

By my right, may the divine spark of the earth, the air, the water,
the fire, and the Spirit in me ignite!
-Tia Johnson

Every Goddess has an element from which she can draw her power. Those elements are earth, air, water, fire, and Spirit. It doesn't matter if you chose to work with more than one element, just as long as you know how to work with the elements. You can involve the elements throughout your daily life. For example, want to be great in something you're passionate about in your life? Invoke the element of fire. Want to be a great communicator? Invoke the element of air. Want to relate to people on an emotional level? Invoke the element of water. Want to level with people and be frank? Invoke the element of earth. Want to appeal to a higher power? Invoke Spirit. To invoke means to call upon positive energies, the deities or other positive energies, to help you in your spiritual work. Also, do not forget to evoke your own energy since you will be boosting your energy through the use of the elements. You can evoke your energy by saying, "I call upon my source energy to be present as I do my spiritual work". Evoking your energy is to call upon your positive energies, internal energy, whereas invoking is involving external energy.

In the example below, write your reactions. Then come back to the reactions a few hours from now and see if you would change those answers.

Connecting with the elements helps you to maintain balance. The great thing about working with the elements is that they are easily accessible. Below are some quick and simple rituals to get in touch with your elements.

Earth Ritual:

My 'Earth Ritual' isn't much of a ritual, but more of a connection. I buy bamboo plants and it is with those bamboo plants that I connect with the earth element. I communicate with the bamboo plants by listening to it when it requests water or if it notifies me when needs trimming for when it begins to turn a bit yellow. In addition, I practice my reiki on the bamboo plants especially when I trim the plants because a piece of that plant is gone and healing is required. As a result, I am able to connect with the earth because I listen to the rhythms of the earth.

Air Ritual:

I love doing is air ritual at night just because I love the night and that 'nighttime air. 'However, you can do this air ritual in the daytime; it is all based on preference. I go outside and look up at the sky and take deep breaths. As I inhale, my eyes are open; as I exhale, I close my eyes and I think of nothing. I just ask goddess Athena to grant me wisdom and enjoy the breezes of the night air. It just feels cleansing. After several deep breaths, I begin to set intentions. Since the element of air deals with wisdom, I tend to set my intentions in regards to achieving sacred knowledge. Of course, you can set your intentions as you see fit for your highest good. While I'm setting my intentions, I imagine that with each inhalation I am receiving knowledge and with each exhalation I am releasing any falsehoods. Thus, I am opening my mind to possibilities and understandings.

Water Ritual:

I do the following water ritual daily, especially when I come home from work. I call it my 'ritual shower'. I find this ritual quick and easy because is a very simple process since you can do it in the comfort and privacy of your own home, not to mention you can take as much time as you like! When I come home from work, I prepare the bathroom for the ritual by asking Archangel Michael to clear the space. Then, I place my iPhone in a secure place in the bathroom and have a playlist playing music (sometimes I burn incense). Next, I get into the shower and create another sacred space by surrounding myself a white light. So, now, it's a sacred space within a sacred space. After I center myself, I invite goddesses Ix Chel and Lakshmi into my sacred space. When I invite them into my sacred space I imagine healing an abundance taking place as well as lower energies is being washed down the drain.

Fire Ritual:

Fire is, by far, my favorite element, with water being my second favorite. Fire is such a powerful and transformative element in which we all can benefit. My favorite place to work with the element of fire is in the sauna. I love it because it is very hot, dark, and mysterious in the sauna. In addition, I get to meditate, detoxify, and connect with fire goddesses like Pele and Freyja. However, if getting to a sauna is not feasible, another ritual I do is imagine a swirl of fire surrounding me. Basically, I am imagining sacred fire in the shape of a spiral starting at my feet going upward towards my head. I am usually sitting down in a lotus position or I have my feet planted firmly on the floor with either my hands folded or my left hand will be open facing downwards and my right hand open facing outward to represent that as above so below axiom. In both cases, I set intentions to be a transformative being, in which I continue to grow spiritually.

Spirit Ritual:

No particular ritual is required to connect with spirit because spirit can be accessed anywhere at any time. Just by doing the rituals above, you are connecting with spirits and spirit encompasses all. Just thinking of connecting with spirit opens the possibilities.

Elements are a Goddess' best friend because they aid in boosting one's creativity, passion, intuition, understanding, healing, connecting with Spirit and so forth.

One way you can ascertain what element a goddess is associated with is by paying attention to the colors she's wearing. For example, Brigit, Freyja, and Lilith are mostly depicted wearing the color red. Therefore, one can ascertain that an element those goddesses work with is fire. Also, goddesses like Ix Chel work with the rainbow and they are all part of Spirit, which is why there isn't a 'Spirit' category listed below.

A Goddess and her elements:

Goddess	Earth	Air	Fire	Water
Isis		♥	♥	♥
Freyja	♥	♥	♥	♥
Quan Yin				♥
Brigit		♥	♥	♥
Athena		♥		
Dana	♥			♥
Kali	♥	♥	♥	♥
Lilith		♥	♥	
Cerridwen				♥
Lakshmi				♥
Aphrodite				♥
Pele			♥	
Ix Chel				♥

Goddess Freyja used the four elements to obtain the mystical necklace Brisingamen, a symbol of splendor, influence, and abundance when one works in balance with the elements. One day, Freyja saw four dwarves, smiths who were called the Brisings, crafting the precious necklace and decided that she had to have that necklace. Since none of the four dwarves would sell the necklace to her, she agreed to their proposal of spending the night with each dwarf; and, in return, she then will receive the necklace.

The four dwarves represent the four elements and the night that she spent with each dwarf represents a ritual she did honoring each element. Thus, she was able to achieve balance, the Brisingamen necklace.

CHAPTER 5
SETTING GOALS

Don't compromise yourself.
You are all you've got.
-Janis Joplin

Every Goddess has goals to accomplish, things she would like to see done. For example, Quan Yin wants to ensure that every person's prayer is answered and that no one will cry. Isis' goal was to restore her husband. Ix Chel's goal is to heal.

There are three areas that commonly hinder people from reaching their goals because they lack they a "will and a way" type of mentality. The three areas are time, money, and knowledge.

There are, in most cases, several goals that have to be accomplished before you can obtain your main goal. That is, you are more likely going to go through point B, C, and D in order to get to point E when starting from point A. The key is to never lose sight of that main goal when one of the smaller goals does not go according to plan.

In 1995 I had $7 bucks in my pocket and knew two things:
I was broke as hell and one day I won't be.
You can achieve anything.
-Dwayne Johnson

You can use your chakras to help you obtain your goals, mainly because what you do will have to resonate with you. Think about it for a minute, if you lie to someone you love, it will not feel right; the same is true when we lie to ourselves by not having goals that align with our Divine purpose. In regards to one's life purpose, if what you do is what you love, then your talents will be enjoyed by those you love. A great way to ensure that you are on the right path is to communicate with your chakras. You're goals will coincide with your chakras because each goal will affect a chakra to some extent. Below is a picture of your chakras and how they relate to several common goals. I would like for you to think about a goal and how it affects your chakras. Your chakras, or wheels of light, deals with your life force energy.

Functions	Chakras	Goals
Claircognizance (knowing/knowledge)	Crown	Gain a better understanding of who you are and who you can become
Clairvoyance (Visions)	Third Eye	Receive visions of the next step of your journey
Communication/Artistic Expression	Throat	Develop new and wonderful ways to express yourself
Love	Heart	Learn to love yourself and others even more
Self-Confidence	Solar Plexus	Learn that you are important and have a purpose
Sexuality	Sacral	Exploring new depths of your sexuality
Survival	Root/Base	Learn to build strong foundations

A chakra is a center of organization that receives, assimilates, and expresses life force energy.
-Eastern Body Western Mind

To obtain a goal is to 'score' in a sense. In many cases, we think of goals made in games in which there is a time limit. Well, I'm here to tell you don't let 'time' be this horrible factor in 'scoring'. Time is not linear. Know that you have as much time as you need. I know what you're thinking, 'Tia, I have children, I'm in school, I'm tired from work', and so forth. Believe me when I tell you that I once had that thought that time is linear and there is not enough time in the day for the things I wanted and needed to do. Before I even thought to communicate with the angels and Merlin to ask for 'time extention' I made time, meaning that I slept little, stayed up all hours of the night working on my projects and yes, I would go to work the next day and function properly. While that may not seem doable to you, it's what worked for me for many of years. Looking back it was mostly likely the angels and Merlin giving me more strength to do what needed to be done. After learning that the angels and Merlin can help me with time and energy, I learned that time is what you make it. An hour can feel like a life time (ask a person who had to wait for the next plane) and a life time can feel like a moment ago (just ask a parent about their adult child).

When working to accomplish your goals, ask the angels and Merlin to give you more than enough time and energy to accomplish your goals. Ask them to help you let go of worrying about time and stamina. You can be conscious about the time, but not worrisome or obsessive.

A true Goddess will not let minor things like 'time' distract her. Use your Goddess abilities, such as calling on the goddesses, seeking the aid of the elements and so forth, to direct your energy to make time work for you and not the other way around. You want to 'own it' and watch how your schedule becomes clear; how people are available to help you, how you accomplish things 'faster', and so on. Three keys are essential here:
- Be open to receiving time and energy in unexpected ways
- Notice signs and symbols, especially if you meet new people
- Be prepared to follow through and take action on the messages you received

Again, the Goddess Isis comes to mind. When her husband was murder by his brother and his body dismembered, she traveled, in many disguises, through Earth and the Underworld to obtain her goal of reuniting with my husband; reassembling him and returning him to life. Isis was able to reassemble her husband, but without his penis, so she created one from gold.

Do you think Isis let a little thing like 'time' stand in the way of her reuniting with her husband? Not a chance! And, when she couldn't locate his penis, she adjusted her plans and 'created' one out of gold.

Throughout your journey, like Isis, you will take on many forms; become a multi-tasker, in order to achieve your goals. Don't let time be the thing to hold you back.

- **Don't let time rule your world**
  - Think affirming thoughts like, 'I have just enough time to get what I need done.'
  - Expect time to work in your favor

Money can easily be another setback, if you allow it to be, in accomplishing your goals. I'm here to explain that the Goddess Lakshmi is more than willing to help a girlfriend! She is the Hindu Goddess of abundance. What you need to know is that the universe is abundant and all you have to do is tap into that flow. How to do it, you may say? Well, see below.

- **Be willing to be open to the endless possibilities**
  - Meaning expect to receive money from unlikely places, people, etc
- **Change your Mindset**
  - In other words, 'positive thought equals positive results'. But, you have to believe. Don't make excuses or 'this is not an excuse but a reason' type of response. Instead, think 'rich'. Don't focus on lack. Look in the mirror and see yourself as an abundant person.
- **Things you need to know**
  - Being rich ≠ being evil just because you see some celeb on some tv network acting out of control, entitled or what have you. They are not you! You can do good things with your money. Money is freedom and you will be free to create many opportunities for others with it.
  - Do I deserve this? Yes you do. Period. Do you need to breathe? Hopefully, you answered yes because you need money like you need to breathe because it's your livelihood!
  - What if people know I'm rich and expect me to change? Who cares! People are going to think what they will anyway. Plus, it's none of your concern how people perceive you, that is their issue. Goddesses fulfill their purpose without the need for everyone to agree.
  - Can I handle large sums of money? Of course you can! And, you can hire a financial planner or accountant to help you manage the money.

❧Respect your money
- Say 'thank you' to even the pennies you have. Buy a nice wallet and spend your money well. When you show appreciation, you tend to receive more. So, have manners.
- Keep the change! Put a few pennies, nickels, dimes, and quarters in your pocket so that you hear it and when you put your hand in your pocket you feel money- this is a signal to you, and the Universe, that you have money. Also, as the saying goes, 'how deep are your pockets?' Well pretty deep because you're carrying a nice amount of change!
- Even though I have been doing the following suggestion since I was kid, I like it and even Oprah suggests it's a good deed: have all your dollar bills facing one way. I just feel like it's good energy going one way.

❧Cleansing your chakras
- Your root chakra is related to material things and foundations. You want to have a positive outlook in regards to money and you want to build a strong foundation with money so that more money will flow your way. A way to cleanse that chakra is to envision a beautiful red rose, located at the base of your spine, blossoming into a rich red color.

Knowledge is another seemly barrier to halt the process of accomplishing goals. In this age of technology, there isn't much that one can't Google or Wikipedia, especially if that certain topic has a Twitter or Facebook page! What I am explaining here is that, in the beginning of your goal process when you are researching what you need to do, you don't have to leave the comfort of your home! It's as if you have an all access VIP pass! Use it!

Athena is the Grecian Goddess of wisdom. Call upon her to help you obtain the wisdom needed to move forward with your journey. One of her symbols is an owl. So, if you happen to come across an owl that's just one way she is letting you know that she hears you and is helping you!

I will tell you that when I started my company, I had just a few hundred dollars in my bank account and I was paying off a lot of credit card debit I had incurred from reckless spending during my college years. I also recently received a raise at my job, but it didn't matter much because I was paying off a lot debt. I had very little holistic tools such as crystals or books. However, I prayed, meditated and connected with my higher self and other divine beings for more money, time, and the ability to make things happen and I believed that it would happen. When you direct your energy to the things you want to accomplish, the Universe will help you. The goddesses will give you the tools you need to complete your tasks. So, don't give up! That's very important. You one day will have a story to tell that will inspire another goddess and it's all thanks to you believing!

I know God will not give me anything I can't handle.
I just wish that He didn't trust me so much.
-Mother Theresa

CHAPTER 6

DEFINING YOUR SYMBOL

Mickey Mouse to me is a symbol of independence.
-Walt Disney

Now, this process does not have to be complicated. It does not have to be a crest with all the trimmings. Instead, it can be as simple as an animal, like an owl or a bear, or mystical, like a dragon or a fairy. Your symbol is something that's your trademark. For example, can you think of a celebrity who wears mainly one colour? Maybe someone you know wears a flower in her hair and has an assortment of the flower accessory. Are you a shoe collector? That is, do you have the same shoe in every colour and a pair of shoes for every possible occasion? Maybe, you prefer charm bracelets or necklaces. How about your tattoos? They can definitely be your symbols!

You don't have to have one symbol. The key here is to have one or several symbols that *represent* you. The meaning of the symbol can be a Traditional meaning like the meaning of an owl being wise or you can put your spin on it by making the owl your symbol because you are a 'night owl'. The colour of your symbol also has a strong meaning so you want to make sure that the colour you choose is right for you but also gets your message across. In addition, you also want to put your energy into this symbol. By doing this, you are literally attaching your vibration to it so when people see that symbol they think of you…think of the symbol of the golden arches. Now, what do you associate with the golden arches? Now, are you hungry for a burger and fries?! Haha.

Goddesses will reveal their symbols to you as confirmation that you are on the right path or that you are close to them and so forth. So, if your path is to start a holistic business to help people with addictions, they may see your company's logo as a sign of support and strength so they won't give into temptations. See how that works?!

So, let create a symbol! If you already have a symbol, then let's elaborate on it by syncing your energy with the symbol! To create a symbol, start with who, what, when, where, why, and how. Below are two exercises, one for those who have a symbol in mind and the other is for those who don't have a symbol in mind. And, remember, a symbol does not have to be something completely physical like a flower. Your symbol can be something slightly abstract like love and then you can create something that reminds you of love.

Love is a symbol of eternity. It wipes out all sense of time,
Destroying all memory of a beginning and all fear of an end.
-Madame de Stael

For those who have a symbol, ask yourself the following; again, just think about it. Don't worry so much about writing out the answers. This is meant to be thought provoking.

What makes it significant?

Who inspired you in your decision (even if you read about a symbol like a book of dragons, the author would be the 'who')?

When did this symbol become of great importance to you?

Where do you foresee the future of the symbol: Maybe make it a logo for your company/hobby?

Where did you discover your symbol?

(If it's a tattoo) Where is it located on your body and why?

How do you plan on making it your signature (maybe showing off the tattoo on the arm by wearing a lot of sleeve-less shirts)?

For those who don't

Name your favorite: animal, flower, color, element, crystal, etc?

Why that animal, flower, color, element, crystal, etc?

How would you explain the symbolic meaning of what you chose as your symbol?

What can you do to the image to add your uniqueness to the symbol?

Where will you have this image?

When did the image first appear to you?

Who inspired you in the creation/picking/etc of the symbol?

Now, let's give your symbol your energy so when people see it they will automatically think of you. Just like the owl is a symbol for the Goddess Athena, representing wisdom. For example, maybe you pick a pink flower. That could symbolize your carefree loving side and when your spouse sees a pink flower he will think of you! So, now that you mentally created a symbol or enhanced your original symbol, let's draw it! Don't worry if you proclaim yourself to be the least creative person in the world. Instead, you can write the word and decorate that word. Below, I described the process I went through in order to develop my company logo.

Tia's thought process in developing The Violet Sanctuary Spa's logo

- My company name is Violet Sanctuary Spa
- The main color is violet with a tint of royal blue and dark purple
- The lotus is a popular flower for spirituality
- The logo has to represent Spirit
- It has to be symmetric
- The number four represents angels and strong foundations
- I have a habit of doodling flowers in my notebooks in school so why not make a flower my icon?!
- See below pictures of one logo that didn't make the cut and the rough draft of the current

logo!

CHAPTER 7
THE DOMAIN IN WHICH YOU REIGN SUPREME

Have the courage to follow your heart and intuition.
They somehow already know what you truly want to become.
Everything else is secondary.
-Steve Jobs

This is it! This is the cherry on top of the icing on top of the cake! And, guess what?! You're not only going to have your cake, but you are going to eat it as well! If we were to look at this book as having two major themes, then your domain would be the second theme, to be goddess would be the first. After going through the previous chapters of rediscovering yourself, you have come to the part where you claim your domain. This is your turf where you are the expert in the subject matter. This is your livelihood, this is *you*.

What do I mean by 'this is you'? Well, you shed new light into your birthday, rediscovered your origins, developed your purpose, sparked your element, achieved your goals, and certified your symbol; basically, you enhanced the story of you; you divine goddess! You recreated your divine profile!

As you become more clear about who you really are,
You'll be better able to decide what is best for you
– the first time around.
-Oprah Winfrey

This is the exact transformation I underwent when I began looking deeper into myself after the death of my grandparents. I know truly in my heart that you will dive deep into your goddess zone and claim your domain! Now, your domain can be one or several things. It's totally up to you! The key here is that you have to be specialized in the area, not to be confused with needing a certification or another form of credibility alone. This also includes life experiences and what knowledge the Goddess has bestowed upon you!

For example, it's awesome to receive certification in an area because it comes with the reputation of credibility. However, can one become a certified parent or grandparent? On the other hand, we need that credential because we need that extra training, that extra experience that will help us along our path; we need that credibility. Being certified definitely goes hand in hand with life experiences and knowledge passed down by the Goddess, but keep in mind that there are some areas that you won't necessarily be certified in, but have a great deal of knowledge to help promote healing.

Also, know that you don't need anyone's permission to conquer your domain. What I'm explaining is that if you know you have a passion to become a lawyer and you want to go as far as becoming a judge in the Supreme Court, you don't need someone to give you the green light to go! Heck, in the beginning you don't need money! You can research at your local library books or borrow a friend's laptop to research what it takes to be a judge.

So, back to discussing your domain in which you reign supreme! In what are you truly *great*? Notice how I emphasized on great and not good. Because this is your domain! You have to be great. I don't want you to confuse being great with being perfect. Being great means you know when to ask for help, you are resourceful, you understand that even if you are the master in an area you are still the student because you are always learning, and you understand that there is always room for more greatness.

> *I've missed more than 9,000 shots in my career. I've lost almost 300 games.*
> *26 times, I've been trusted to take the game winning shot and missed.*
> *I've failed over and over and over again in my life. And that is why I succeed.*
> *-Michael Jordan*

I use myself as an example. I have the rare ability to listen to people and NOT provide my opinion until it is asked. How often can a person go to a friend, a co worker, etc and actually get a chance to finish their story without the listener being bias or tuning out so that they can provide their answer? My guess is not often enough! I understand that people, more times than not:

- Just want to be heard
- Just want to be understood
- Already know the answers but want to say it out loud or looking for confirmation
- Want to be able to talk without thinking, 'will I be judged?'
- Just want to talk

So, what's my domain? Well, I can call it whatever I like, such as domain of understanding and free talk, domain of the ear chakra, domain of listen now talk later, domain of counsel, and the list goes on! Don't over think this process of owning your domain or naming your domain. Don't compare yourself to someone else who you think is an expert. Remember everyone is on their own path and you cannot possibility know everything there is to know on any particular subject. So, take a deep breath. Ahhh or Ohmmm! And, think about what you are truly great at and then give that domain a name, be as creative as you like! See below for a few amazing tips. I named it as goddess because you are a goddess and what you are great at will be dubbed that name plus goddess!

GREAT AT	POSSIBLE DOMAIN NAME
SEXUAL GODDESS	DOMAIN OF SENSUALITY
PARTY GODDESS	DOMAIN OF CELEBRATION
LISTENING GODDESS	DOMAIN OF COMPASSION
FASHION GODDESS	DOMAIN OF DESIGN
MAKING GOOD JUDGEMENT GODDESS	DOMAIN OF ATHENA
HOLIDAY GODDESS	DOMAIN OF 'TIS THE SEASON
MAKEUP GODDESS	DOMAIN OF EXPRESSION
JUDO GODDESS	DOMAIN OF FIGHT CLUB
TRAVEL GODDESS	DOMAIN OF PARADISE
MOMMY GODDESS	DOMAIN OF THE TRIPLE MOON
COOKING GODDESS	DOMAIN OF DELIGHT
BAD ASS GODDESS	DOMAIN OF I WILL TAKE NO SHIT
SPORTY GODDESS	DOMAIN OF GOOD COMPETITION
BUSINESS GODDESS	DOMAIN OF BUSINESS RELATIONS
WICCAN GODDESS	DOMAIN OF THE ANCIENT WAYS
TATTOO GODDESS	DOMAIN OF CREATIVE EXPRESSION

GREAT AT	POSSIBLE DOMAIN NAME
WARRIOR GODDESS	DOMAIN OF DETERMINATION
DANCING GODDESS	DOMAIN OF PHYSICAL EXPRESSION
WINE GODDESS	DOMAIN OF CHEERS
SURF GODDESS	DOMAIN OF POSSIBILITIES
TALKATIVE GODDESS	DOMAIN OF MASS COMMUNICATION
NEGOTIATING GODDESS	DOMAIN OF BEING REASONABLE
HEALING GODDESS	DOMAIN OF CONNECTING WITH SELF
SOCIAL MEDIA GODDESS	DOMAIN OF TECHNOLOGY

A wonderful hit song from the 90's come to mind, which helped me to really think about 'where I belong' and where I was going. That song is 'The Sign' by Ace of Base. I was in Montreal, Canada, with friends for a Jazz Festival and one night we decided to go to a karaoke bar. One of my friends picked 'The Sign' to sing, not only did I remember how much I loved this childhood song, I remember the feeling it gave me while listening to it as a child, but I didn't quite get the meaning of it back then and I thought it was I saw the 'sun' not 'sign'! However, it made all of the sense when I was in that little karaoke bar signing my heart out! Even though I was supposed to be on vacation, my mind is always thinking about a million things. I thought about where I belong in my domain, how I can achieve new heights, and how I can help others. Very profound!

CHAPTER 8
CREATING YOUR EPIC JOURNEY

How wonderful it is that nobody need wait a
single moment before starting to improve the world.
-Anne Frank

Why, exactly, are you reading this book? If the answers truly lie within, then why is there a need for this book? Well, because this book is part of your spiritual journey, helping you recall what is already within. This is an on-going conversation between me and you, between you and the goddess. Imagine us sitting at a table in your kitchen drinking cinnamon tea and you're wondering how you can tap into all the power that lies inside of you just begging to come out. And, I say close your eyes, put your dominant hand on your third eye and create a story about yourself, about how you got to this point. Why do I mention 'create' and not 'tell'? Because, to just tell will make your journey technical and you may inadvertently leave out the good parts.

To create allows your imagination to kick in; thus, triggering your subconscious to bring more things to light about your journey to this point. And, this will help you to acknowledge how your story is great; great in a sense that extraordinary things took place in your life that make you, you. You will understand that you do have a story to tell and it's legendary, completely unique to only you! You will also see, on a large scale, how your journey plays a role in shaping the world in which we live!

This is the great story of you, my friend. Every God and Goddess has a great story. What's your story? Grab a hand mirror and look deep into your eyes and take several deep breaths from the stomach. Now, tell the epic story of you. Say it out loud! Let yourself *feel* the emotions of the story and release the things that need to be released. Experiencing trouble in regards to *where* to begin with your story? Well ask yourself about a day in particular where you experienced something that seemed out of the ordinary, such as seeing sparkles, angels, fairies, leprechauns or just knowing about something ahead of time that left a lasting impact, or maybe you had a dream that later came true. Whatever the case, you can start from there and work your way up to the present.

Now, think about something that's common like work. How does your job play into your spiritual journey and on a larger scale, tapping deeper into your inner Goddess? Consider this; you are working at a job that you no longer like. The energy is harsh at this job and you realized after several years there that it no longer suits you. Perhaps this job as a prerequisite to your ultimate mission, a place where you are learning about the harsh energies so that you know how to protect yourself from that energy. In addition, the 'day job' is what will fund your spiritual studies, such as taking certification courses, and this way you can focus on service and not making money because you have money! Now, as a Goddess, you will develop a sense of direction in life. This does not mean that you will always know the destination or that you will even see the entire path. What it means is that you know when you are on the right track because your intuition is your navigation system. Signs and symbols will have meaning now. So when you see the time is 4:44 just as you were in deep thought you know that the angels are supporting you in your decisions and so forth.

Let's think of a few things that make an epic story! Think about how the examples below represent an aspect of your epic journey. Where it applies, associate a person or people to each of the words above, starting with you as the hero/heroine.

In an epic journey, there usually is:
- A hero
- A villain
- Tragedy
- Triumph
- Failure
- Discovery
- Betrayal
- Honor
- Power struggle
- Ultimate victory
- Loss of friends
- Gain of friends
- Gain self-knowledge/strength

Life is a journey not a destination.
 -*Saint Therese of Lisieux*

Think of the movies you have seen that are based on an epic journey. There is usually a narrator. Why? Because so much has to be explained, how the hero is feeling and thinking, what's going on in the background, the impact of others actions in the situation, and the possible uphill battle that's going to soon take place. So, narrate your epic journey as you are creating your epic journey! Say it out loud before your write it down.

Give your journey character as if it's a blockbuster movie! You will notice patterns in your life, symbolisms, great things that have taken place, things that can take place and so much more! Then write it all down, without judgment. Afterwards, leave the writings alone and do not look at them for a day or more. When you do come back to your writings, reread it out loud and quietly. Now, think about how far you have come, what you have accomplished, what you have overcome, and what you will be accomplishing next. Now, imagine if you were to turn all that great information into a book! You can be an inspirational author!

CHAPTER 9
B.A.R.N.

(BOUNDARIES, ALLIES, RESENTMENT, AND NETWORKING)

Be who you are and say what you feel, because those who mind
Don't matter and those who matter don't mind.
-Dr. Seuss

A good socialite will have a few 'connections' and 'acquaintances'; however, a great Goddess would have mastered the skill of networking and forming allies, to set boundaries and be prepared for those who resent her.

Set boundaries:

Your time is valuable and everyone needs to realize this. How to let people know how valuable your time is to you? Well, make yourself scarce from time to time:

- Do not allow yourself to be available all of the time. Use phrases such as, 'I'll be with you shortly I just have to finish___' or 'I'll have to do some research and get back to you' (so you're not running like a mad woman to get the information) Or walk to the printer or another place while talking so that the person sees that you are busy and will talk faster, or at least get to the point!
- Look busy!
- Don't answer your phone right away or all of the time
- Make sure you don't waste your time either! Learn how to make your points clear and concise
- When at home, tell the children mom needs 'her time to unwind from a busy day and I'll be with you after I shower.'
- Your husband, wife, boyfriend, girlfriend should already understand – that is, if you have already communicated that to them.
- If a friend is taking up all of your time by talking about their problems, then try changing the subject, and if that doesn't work, don't pick up the phone as much or explain to them that it's just too draining to talk about problems all of the time. Then ask them to say something positive

like describing something good that recently happened.

Forming Allies:

Not necessarily your 'best friends', but your allies are people with whom you have formed a type of 'connection' from which you both benefit. For example, you're running in a fundraiser race, you meet a few good people, and you encourage each other throughout the race. Maybe afterwards you add them as a friend on Facebook. Nothing too serious, but if you decide to enter another race you'll keep them in mind and ask if they would like to team up to do another run. Basically, your 'allies' are the 'neutral' friends you will make throughout your life. There is that mutual understanding that you will communicate in regards to a particular subject, for the most part, nothing more, nothing less and that's okay because you will have different friends for different things. The key here is that there is a mutual admiration and understanding. Whereas, for someone who has a 'connect' it's really just a favor being done and usually one person benefits more than the other.

Another example of an ally would be your co-workers. Some of your co-workers will be your great buddies and you don't mind seeing them outside of work; I am not referring to those type co-workers as your allies. I'm referring to those with whom you communicate regularly to complete a task; they aren't exactly your friends, but you have a relationship with them. You'll form a good rapport with them, things are cordial and there is an understanding of your role and their role in the matter, and from time to time personal conversations will arise, such asking how was your weekend and how's the family. Again, the relationship is pretty neutral, there is a mutual understanding of each person's role in the relationship, the atmosphere is cordial, you're most likely the 'go to' person for things, and the relationship rarely goes beyond what was 'established.'

It is because that you are such a versatile goddess that you will be forming these types of allies because you will be meeting amazing people as you fulfill your purpose and that's okay. It's great to know the roles of people in your life because then you know how to treat them! For example, if your boss is an ally, you have that neutral friendship; chances are that you will not be asking her if she wants to check out the local art gallery with you this weekend! No, because it's that mutual understanding that she's the boss and you are the subordinate. However, you would ask one of your close friends who loves art to go with you.

As a goddess, having allies are about understanding that 'neutral' friendship or relationship zone and using that understanding so that you and the people with whom you are communicating will reach a common goal to benefit all, such as working with people in different departments to complete a project. Therefore, don't take anything personal, especially while at work! Your allies do not know you personally. They do not know your favorite food, your spouse's name, the breed of your dog, the car you drive, the music you like and so forth. These are not your personal relationships, but they serve an important purpose in your life so be thankful for them.

Prepare for Resentment:
There will be people who would love to see you rise to the top. There are people who want you to succeed, just not to surpass them. And, then there are people who don't want you to succeed at all. What can you do about the above? Just prepare for it! As a Goddess who is tuning into the ultimate feminine energy through promoting love, healing, nurturing, and so forth, you don't have time to waste on people who don't want you to succeed or just want you to half succeed. Instead of engaging with their negativity, you send them blessings, surround yourself with protective energy, and move on with your life. When confronted, no need to loose composure, you acknowledge that they are just unhappy people.

Therefore, you tell them so! For example, you would say, 'I don't know why you are so concerned about me not succeeding, but clearly there are some internal issues with yourself that you haven't let go. I send blessings your way and pray that you find peace.' Whoa! What a curveball right! On the other hand, there are times when you have to be more blunt and put people in their place. In that case, go with your intuition on what you should do. But, I always suggest taking at least one deep breath before you respond because that allows logic to enter your mind when you're very irate. Thus, you would more likely curve your initial thought to hit that person. Some things aren't worth it, such as getting physical, but what is worth it is letting that person know that you will not take their shit!

Why fight fire with fire, when, in actually, we put fire out by using water. The element of water is in relation to emotions. You want to be emotionally sound. As I stated above, I don't want you throwing punches when someone approaches you the wrong way.

Yes, there are some aggressive Goddesses but those Goddesses are aggressive because they fight for what they believe in or they are the bringers of change. They would not bother to argue with someone who is jealous or narrow minded! So, stay graceful and then let go of those emotions from that person.

You may also experience resentment because you are becoming more powerful. Thus, people who you used to hang out with may fade into the background because they can no longer 'deal' with you. Don't you feel out of place either because the people who you used to hang out with were good for that particular time in your life. Now, it's time for change, which is fine because you will be attracting more equally strong, positive people! People may develop ideas about you or give you a new 'name' because you're this new strong woman. You may experience the following changes within yourself:

1. Know want you want
2. Stand your ground
3. Very detailed in your work and won't leave until you're satisfied
4. Change your look
5. Will not settle for less
6. Petty things no longer bother you
7. You become more of a visionary
8. You no longer fear change
9. You work with goddesses all the time
10. Your world is your domain…you call the shots
11. Manifesting is easy for you
12. You will radiate golden energy
13. Your posture will change
14. People will notice that you've changed
15. You will be in sync with money, time, and knowledge
16. You have a better understanding of the universe and how it works
17. Your diet will change since you're high vibrational; thus, you will drop excess weight

The new 'name' I was referring to earlier, we all heard it before. Strong women *earn* or are *dubbed* the name or names from people who don't necessarily respect them (of course this is granted that the strong woman is not rude). Three names that come to mind are bitch, diva, and over achiever. If you know what you want, are firm, stand your ground, expect to be respected, and so forth, then some people consider you to be a bitch. If you are high-maintenance, care how you look, won't settle for less, then some people consider you to be a diva. If you are detailed in your work, care, and have a passion for what you do then some people consider you to be an over achiever.

Well, ladies, in ancient times, to be called a 'bitch' was a sign of sacredness, respect, and honor. In order to honor Athena, her priestesses filled her temple with dogs who howled at the moon. Her priestesses were also known as holy bitches. Artemis, goddess of the hunt, was also called Great Bitch and led a pack of hunting priestesses who were referred to as *sacred bitches*. It wasn't until other religions began their 'missions' that these temple priestess bitches became the derogatory term we know it to be today. So, next time someone calls you a 'bitch' say 'thank you'. Now, let's put an even more positive spin on the term *bitch*.

I AM	I AM	I AM	I AM a
Beautiful	Bold	Breath-taking	Boss
Inspirational and a	Inspiring	Important	Intelligent
Talented	Tenacious	Trust-worthy	Teacher
Champion of	Complete	Caring	Charitable
Herself	Honorable	Hypnotic	Healthy

YOUR TURN

(say it out loud or to yourself and yes do it four times because that's the number of angelic help and of solid foundations and we want to built a solid foundation with these words)

I AM A	I AM A	I AM A	I AM A
B	B	B	B
I	I	I	I
T	T	T	T
C	C	C	C
H	H	H	H

The origin of the word diva is Italian, which translates to goddess, from Latin feminine of divus divine, god. Diva also means a glamorous and successful female performer or personality. The synonyms for diva are goddess, princess, and queen. Now, *diva* is not such a bad word! So, let's put our own definition to the word *diva*!

I AM A	I AM A	I AM	I AM
Divine	Delightful	Delicious	Devoted
Individual who	Inquisitive	Intense	Illuminating
Values	Vivacious	Valuable	Vocal
All	Admired	Adored	Approachable

YOUR TURN

I AM A	I AM A	I AM A	I AM A
D	D	D	D
I	I	I	I
V	V	V	V
A	A	A	A

Throughout school, we are encouraged, almost inundated, with thoughts of being the best we can be to the best of our abilities. Then at some point in our lives we realize that our best just is not good enough. Then what? Well, we tend to go through this period of 'why bother' and 'wtf'. Some of us want to do better, rectify the mistakes, and so forth. We tend to become the dreaded *over achiever*. Maybe we are that type A personality who wants to make sure that everything is done correctly and detail is accounted for. Either way, people who tend to be more relaxed in certain areas tend to dub others as the over achiever. Of course, this is granted that the person is not being a crazed micromanager etc. So, let's reinvent the term *over achiever*!

I
Overtly
Value
Energy
Resilience

And
Chooses
Her
Individuality as
Extremely
Valuable and
Ever
Reliable

YOUR TURN

(One here is fine since it's long)

I AM
O
V
E
R

A
C
H
I
E
V
E
R

Remember, everything on this planet is vibrational, including words. If we become more conscious of the words we use and how we use them, then we won't be affected so much by those who mean harm by using words against us.

The skill of networking:

How do you define 'networking'? One can be a great social media expert and make a great networker that way. Others are great speakers and can hold a great conversation, making them, also, great networkers. I'm going to discuss networking in regards to promoting you! As a goddess, developing the skill of networking is key to your development because you will be the expert in one or several areas in which people will come to your for consulting; however, there will be times when you will have to recommend someone, possibly an ally, due to their expertise and vice versa.

Networking is another way in which people will discover you. You will have to promote yourself and with the great services you will provide, people will highly recommend you! You have to believe in yourself, but not be overbearing. Do away with the idea of thinking promoting yourself is wrong or just do minimum promotions. Have you heard of any successful person doing mini promos? Successful people have no problem telling you what they do for a living and how good they are in their career. It's not showing off, it is being confident and having an understanding that they may be talking to their protégé!

Networking is a great way to get people to understand who you are, what you do, and how you plan to help. Be confident and know it's okay to want to receive payment for holistic services that you have rendered; what you offer is valuable to people. Some people may berate you for being firm in your networking process and setting up a payment structure, but hold your ground! You have to earn a living, you deserve to receive credit, and the world needs to know that you're awesome!

Invoke Lilith, the Hebrew goddess of great strength, to help you to stand your ground and remain strong. Lilith, the first wife of Adam, was created at the same time and the same way, from the Earth, as Adam. When she refused Adam's demand to be his subservient, she left the Garden of Eden and fled to the shores of the Red Sea. It is because of her so called 'defiance' that she 'earned' the title of being a 'she-devil'. Nevertheless, Lilith stood her ground, remained strong, and was not sorry for her actions, never allowing others misrepresentations of her affect her true nature.

The Garden was too restrictive to her; she wanted to become queen of her own domain.
-The Goddess Pages

Lilith's Decree

By my own powers, I will not fall to the wayside of living a life where I am to remain in the passenger's seat.

I blaze my own trail and it is through my trail that I will inspire others to live the life they were meant to live, not told or strongly suggested.

I embrace my sexuality because it's natural, it's innate, and it's meant to flourish.

I am who I am.

I love and I live.

To be strong and determined is not to be vain and spiteful.

I cannot concern myself with such lower matters

For I am divinely inspired

PART III

The Goddess You Will Continue To Be

Do What Ye Will

And

Harm None

CHAPTER 1
MIRROR, MIRROR, ON THE WALL, WHO IS THE GODDESS OF THEM ALL

If you have a candle, the light won't glow any dimmer if I light yours off of mine.
-Steven Tyler

You are the best and there is no one like you; however, you can share your domain!

You are a great Goddess. If you made it to this chapter, without skipping ahead, then you just about have your complete Goddess biography. Therefore, you have realized even more of your gifts, making you an even more powerful Goddess.

Go ahead, look in the mirror. What do you truly see? Grab a mirror and look deep into your eyes and follow the below Deep Insight Exercise:

- Take 5 deep breaths (five because it's the number for change)
- Close your eyes and count to ten
- Now, open your eyes and just stare into them

Think:
- Who am I?
- How do I feel?
- What is it that I am feeling?
- When I look deep into my eyes, what do I see?
- When I look deep into my eyes, what do I feel?
- Am I *really* living my life?
- Why am I here?
- Do I have a better understanding of my purpose?

- What do I have a passion for?

Know that every Goddess you come across is a reflection of you in one form or another. The Goddess is multifaceted like a diamond, but it's still one diamond, one spirit. You are one 'facet' of the diamond. You can share your domain, meaning that if your realm is the realm of cooking, it doesn't mean someone else cannot be a great cook. They are just a different cook. By sharing your domain, you're actually inviting people in your life to share your goodwill! For example, a mother who is a great cook will teach her daughter the 'family recipes' by inviting her in the kitchen and teaching her how to cook.

There are endless benefits from sharing your domain on both a personal and a business level. We can share our domain by teaching others traits we learned and working with fellow professionals to achieve the even greater goal of making the world a better place! Below are just a few ways in which sharing your domain is beneficial.

- We learn lessons from each other; thus gaining 'experience points'
- We will one day become the mentor
- We will get to meet people of the same trade/make friends/network
- We will reap the benefits of the law of giving and receiving
- We build trust
- We will feel happy knowing that we helped someone
- We will feel happy explaining to someone what we do
- Sharing creates a feeling of abundance

Also remember that you never know whose life you may affect with your positive attitude. You don't know what people are going through even if that person is smiling. So, when you have an award-wining attitude as a goddess who cares and is willing to show others the tricks of the trade, it's awesome!

The best example that comes to mind are the television cooks, they invite fellow cooks and bakers to come on their program to show some of their famous foods! There's no threat or other worries about one cook being better than another and 'stealing' television ratings.

To have the ability to share your domain means that you are comfortable within your surroundings and confident with yourself to a degree where you do not feel intimidated by others. Remember, the Universe is abundant and you are in abundance. Therefore, there is no need to sabotage others or refuse to help others who want to do great things and be a great person. Instead, it's more of a compliment to you for helping them to succeed! It shows that you have character!

In order to help you get into the mindset of knowing that you are in abundance, you can work with the Hindu goddess of abundance, Lakshmi.

Lakshmi's Decree

Abundance surrounds,

Abundance abound

The gourd of abundance is ever present and never ending.

Light like a lotus flowing on the water, abundance comes to me like a gentle wave.

I recognize symbols and take action to achieve my goals.

Goddess Lakshmi, let your golden light radiate around me as I absorb it and soak in its goodness

What I receive in abundance I also give in abundance.

I dance in abundance because I honor the sacredness of the abundant Universe.

CHAPTER 2
INVOKING THE GODDESS AND GODDESS RITUALS

The location is of no importance so long as the connection is there.
-Tia Johnson

Recruit the Goddesses! Through working with these goddesses, you will discover which one or ones work closely with you! Below are the thirteen goddesses that we have been working with throughout this book and an aspect of that goddess to be used in the following rituals. I suggested simple supplies so that the process would be more focused on connecting with the goddesses than figuring out where to purchase certain items or whether or not one item can be substituted for another that cannot be obtained. The main focus is to ascertain which goddess or goddesses you resonate most with and work with that goddess or goddesses, and learn more about yourself! Just to keep it simple, I listed quick and simple phrases for you to invoke each goddess

Before you begin any of the rituals, make sure the surrounding space is clear by asking Archangel Michael, the chief protector angel, to clear your space. Then center yourself by taking several deep breaths. Of course, your ritual can be as intricate or as simple as you like. However, if you were anything like me in the beginning of my spiritual studies, simplicity is best until you are more comfortable with the more intricate rituals.

While working with the goddesses, keep in mind that each of them has their own vibration. Therefore, you may fill a strong energy or a soft energy. Remember to relax and be willing to receive visions, messages, feelings, and so forth. Also, keep in mind that the goddesses will continue to connect with you throughout the day. So, you may see more of an image that is related to a particular goddess. The main factor is the keep an open mind because the possibilities of how you will connect with the goddesses are unlimited

Isis - Divine Magic

What you will require:

- A picture of Isis or the triple moon symbol
- A white candle and meditation music
- Invoke Isis by saying, 'I invoke you, goddess Isis into my sacred space to grant me the understanding of divine magic.'

Freyja – Sex Goddess

What you will require:

- A picture of Freyja or of a lion
- A red candle and meditation music
- Invoke Freyja by saying, 'I invoke you goddess Freyja, into my sacred space to grant me the understanding of divine sex magic.'

Quan Yin-Compassion

What you will require:

- A picture of Quan Yin or of a lotus
- A soft colored candle like pink and meditation music
- Invoke goddess Quan Yin by saying, 'I invoke you goddess Quan Yin, into my sacred space to grant me the power of compassion.'

Bridgit- Illumination

What you will require:

- A picture of Bridgit or of a lit candle
- A red candle or a white candle
- Invoke goddess Brigit by saying, 'I invoke you goddess Brigit, into my sacred space to grant me the ability to illuminate my path.'

Athena-Wisdom

What you will require:

- A picture of Athena or of a fig
- A green, white, or blue candle
- Invoke goddess Athena by saying, 'I invoke you goddess Athena, into my sacred space to grant me the power of wisdom.'

Dana- Manifestation

What you will require:

- A picture of Dana or of elves/fairies/leprechauns
- A dark green candle
- Invoke goddess Dana into your sacred space by saying, 'I invoke you goddess Dana, into my sacred space to grant me the ability to be a great manifestor.'

Kali- Understanding Life Cycles

What you will require:

- A picture of Kali or of the dark (new) moon
- A black or purple candle
- Invoke goddess Kali into your sacred saying, 'I invoke you goddess Kali, into my sacred space to grant me the ability to understand and appreciate life cycles.'

Lilith- Stand in Your Belief; Be an Individual

What you will require:

- A picture of Lilith or of a snake
- A red or black candle
- Invoke goddess Lilith into your sacred space by saying, 'I invoke you goddess Lilith, into my sacred space to grant me the power to uphold my beliefs for my highest good.'

Cerridwen- Dealing with Transformation

What you will require:

- A picture of Cerridwen or of a cauldron
- A white or silver candle
- Invoke Cerridwen into your sacred space by saying, 'I invoke you goddess Cerridwen, into my sacred space to grant me the ability to transform me and my world.'

Lakshmi- Accepting Abundance

What you will require:

- A picture of Lakshmi or of golden coins
- A yellow or white candle
- Invoke goddess Lakshmi into your sacred space by saying, 'I invoke you goddess Lakshmi, into my sacred space to grant me the ability to see the abundance that's already in my world and the ability to attract more abundance.

Aphrodite- Accepting and Receiving Love

What you will require:

- A picture of Aphrodite or of pearls/open clam
- A pink, red, blue, or white candle
- Invoke goddess Aphrodite into your sacred space by saying, 'I invoke you goddess Aphrodite, into my sacred space to grant me the ability to see the love that's already in my world, to attract more love into my world, and to be able to accept and receive love from a balanced state.'

Pele- Igniting Your Divine Flame

What you will require:

- A picture of Pele or of an erupting volcano
- A red, orange, or yellow candle
- Invoke goddess Pele into your sacred space by saying, 'I invoke you goddess Pele, into my sacred space to grant me the ability to ignite my Divine Flame. May I have the passion for life, to live it to the fullest, to be of service, and excel in my spiritual domain.'

Ix Chel- Accepting and Receiving Healing

What you will require:

- A picture of Ix Chel of a rainbow/Mayan pyramid
- A green or white candle (since the rainbow is associated with Ix Chel a collection of candles is acceptable)
- Invoke goddess Ix Chel into your sacred space by saying, 'I invoke you goddess Ix Chel, into my sacred space to grant me the ability to be a superb healer and to be able to accept healing.'

CHAPTER 3
CHANNELED MESSAGES FROM THE GODDESS

Meditation is listening to the Divine within.
-Edgar Cayce

As a distinct way to dive into your Goddess energy, meditate with the Goddess and amplify the power of meditation with a crystal, such as a clear quartz! The answers have always been within you, in some cases being dormant just waiting for you to activate their power; and in other cases, just waiting for you to perfect their power. Before I did the meditation to receive these messages, I asked the goddesses "what are some things that we do every day and don't realize that it's the goddess within us?" I thought of this question because I remember when my grandmother would sweep the living room, but sweep the contents outside of the house! She literally would sweep the dust right outside. As a kid at the time, I just had written it off as something 'grandmothers do'. But, now, having understanding of the meaning of a broom as a way to 'cleanse the house', I can understand that whether she knew it or not, my grandmother was physically and spiritually cleansing the house!

Below are terms and their definitions which were given to me while in deep meditation with the Goddesses:

1. **The Goddess wave:**
   Usually used as A Great Welcoming and as a means to lift the energy of a person, place, or thing. A wave (physically with the hand or hands) of positive energy sent to people, places, and things. Not to be confused with just a wave to another person to signify your location or just to say 'hi'.

2. **The Goddess Powerball:**
   A ball of Goddess energy, extremely light and extra loving like a bubble. Usually used to send loving, healing, energy.

3. **The Goddess Wrath:**

A very strong psychic attack. Usually done when she feels betrayed. Note: Not all Goddesses emit the Goddess Wrath.

4. **Goddess Protection:**

Love and light defense energy usually by means of a simple kiss. Similar to when mothers kiss their kids on the forehead. By kissing the forehead, the mother is granting the child foresight, to notice the surroundings especially if it's bad. When kissed on the top of the head, to help the child to know when to do the right thing, even if it means going against their friends. When holding and kissing the hands, to help the children to be grateful when receiving. I received a vision of a mother kissing her adolescent child on the top of his head while he leaves to go to school.

5. **Sex of The Goddess:**

Intense sexual energy. Very spiritual. The Goddess does not necessarily have to 'touch' a person. Her energy alone emits intense passion on multiple levels. She psychically announces her arrival and people just feel and become attracted to whatever energy she sends.

6. **Work of the Goddess:**

The purpose or purposes the Goddess chooses to be part of; such as love, to nature, healing, change, abundance, etc.

7. **Romantic Kiss of the Goddess:**

Exchanging of energies. Very physical. The process of opening up of the Goddess's lover chakras (kundalini) in order to experience more of the Goddess on a physical level. The Goddess infuses her energy with her lovers, further ensuring that they are connected. This is one reason why some people are hesitant to kiss, but are willing to do other things. The 'kiss' will ignite not only a union, but also cell memory will be activated. So, if there is a past life associated with the Goddess and her love, there will be a 'jog of memory' so to speak.

8. **Touch of the Goddess:**

    Energy impulses the Goddess sends mainly to induce healing. Similar to Reiki, but mainly the Goddess Golden Light is used. This is usually done when the Goddess is in the same area of the person receiving the healing.

9. **The Golden Goddess:**

    When a woman reaches her ultimate Goddess realization. She will radiate a golden aura which can be either felt, seen, or both by all. This does not necessarily mean that she has unlocked all of her Goddess powers; instead it means that she has realized her potential and is on her way to achieving this accordingly.

10. **Heart of the Goddess:**

    When a Goddess devotes herself to a lover for a period of time either known or unknown. This does not mean that the lover 'belongs' to the Goddess or that the Goddess 'belongs' to the lover. Instead, this is a formal commitment that the Goddess is in love with the lover and not using the lover. It is the highest gift one can receive from the Goddess, besides a child, because to receive the Heart of the Goddess means the lover's vibration, soul, etc is propelled to a higher frequency and their life purpose will become even clearer. Note: to receive a child from the Goddess, either through natural causes or adoption, is a high gift because her energy is in the child and she trusts you with that energy, to help the child grow and do great things.

11. **High Gift of the Goddess:** A child or children. It does not matter if the child or children were adopted because the Goddess will still pour her energy into the children, making them her children. This is a high gift of the Goddess because she is trusting you with something very sacred.

12. **Gift of the Goddess:**

    Any gift the Goddess gives you, other than her heart and a child(ren) because they are the high gifts. However, it's typically love, protection, and good fortune.

13. Harmonics of the Goddess:

An otherworldly tune a Goddess hums. The tune can promote whatever the Goddess wishes, such as instant healing.

14. Soul of the Goddess:

The connection between all Goddess; all Goddesses are one, one entity in many forms.

15. Eye of the Goddess:

When a Goddess gazes deeply into a person's eyes, usually a lover or someone with whom she is attracted, she is no longer using her physical eyes to make a simple connection. Instead, she is using her mind's eye to connect with one's soul. She is using her Goddess eye to use her energy to fully relate to you on an indescribable level. The focus here is to reach a point of understanding without a shadow of doubt of what is going to take place, such as sex or a passionate kiss.

CHAPTER 4
ADORING THE EVERYDAY GODDESS

Love yourself first and everything else falls into line.
You really have to love yourself to get anything done in this world.
-Lucille Ball

Adoring yourself is the best gift you can give yourself and others. Very typical, not to mention free, daily activities are beneficial for you. Typical things like getting a manicure and pedicure and free things like going to a park, writing yourself a love letter, and talking to people are all examples of how adoring the everyday goddess can be done.

Here's why manicures and pedicures are important (yes, even if you are a man you can get pedicures and manicures. It will show that you take extra care of yourself!):

- It's one of those ultimate self care activities you can do for yourself because you are literally taking a backseat and letting someone else take control while you relax
- You can be as creative as you want and get seasonal, vibration colours or keep it simple with a French manicure.
- You'll get your chakras in gear because most likely, especially if you frequent the place, you will chat (throat chakra) and meet new people, show appreciation and genorsity by giving a tip and saying thank you (heart chakra), or just getting it done for something special like date night (sacral and root chakra).
- Note: If you are sensitive to chemicals at the nail salon, then you can get the nail art kits that allow you to press on nails with art designs or provide you with tools to do your own nails/nail design. You can do your nails with your girlfriend, daughter, and so forth to achieve that level of interaction.

Do a few 'park visitations' and write love letters:
- Love dogs? Go to a dog park! It's so therapeutic. There's a dog park I frequent and it's just so lovely to see the dogs play with each other!

- Visit a historical park, if possible. I'm located in Philadelphia, so there are loads of historic, and sometimes hidden, parks. One of my favorite parks incorporated all of the elements, there's a fire pit, a water fountain, loads of trees, wonderful breezes, and, of course, spirit is everywhere.
- Write a love letter to yourself by addressing a letter to you and write all the reasons why you're just the awesome person you are and will continue to be throughout your life. Afterwards, mail the letter! What you just did was send your awesome love out into the Universe and it will return to you! Won't you just be delighted to receive something so awesome! Heck, spray the letter with your favorite perfume!
- Write the love letters to yourself throughout the year!

Entertain the thought…

- Grab a friend, go to a hair supply store, and try on a few crazy color wigs just to get your mind to entertain the thought of being a bit silly and imaginative. By doing this, you are tapping into your child-like imagination of what it would be like if…
- Buy an outfit that's a bit daring and compliments your body type at the same time; redefine the little black dress. By doing this, you entertain the thought of being the hottest woman trotting her stuff! You don't have to wear the outfit outside (at first!). This is to get you in the mindset that you are worth it, whatever 'it' may be to you! Don't look for others to compliment you. Compliment yourself! Go right to that mirror and say, 'I'm a sexy goddess; that's right!'

Meditate regularly and throughout the day to keep you positive and give you a boost of energy! Your meditations can be as intricate or simple. It's all up to you! Going to an interview or meeting? Do a quick meditation to remain level headed by taking several deep breaths and imagine angel lights surrounding you, keeping your thoughts beautiful and keeping your body language relaxed.

When you wake up in the morning, do a goddess devotion. For example, you can say, 'I am a true goddess and I honor myself each day' and then imagine what that means to you. Next, think about how you take care of your body. Also, keep in mind that as your vibration raises so it will be in tune with your inner goddess, it's very likely that you will have to switch to more organic/ sensitive skin products. I had to because my skin started to have an adverse reaction to certain soaps,

deodorants, and, especially, detergents.
- What type of soaps you use for your body?
- What exfoliate do you use for your body? I actually use a sea salt mixture for my face and the rest of my body.
- What perfumes do you use for your body? I spray the perfume at a distance.
- Do you drink a lot of water and eat a lot of fruit? Eat and drink the amounts that you feel is right. The goddesses will guide you. Don't force yourself to drink loads of water and eat loads of fruit; do it in moderation.
- Do you bless your food and water?
- Do you tune up your body via reiki and other healing modalities?
- Do you make time for rest? Don't use the phrase 'take time' because you are suggesting that you don't have time; and, therefore, must 'take it'. This is a 'biggie' for me because I love what I do; I forget to make time for breaks! I feel like I can go on forever!
- Who loves your body? You, your boyfriend/girlfriend husband/wife? You better say you love your body!
- How often do you exercise?
- What do you do when you exercise?
- Where do you exercise? Note: What I realized is that the gym is the most narcissistic place on the planet, but in a good way. No one is judging you, at least not at my gym! I have seen people who are very much so in shape, others who aren't, and a few in between. I've seen people wear nice, color coordinated, gym clothes, while others just threw on something loose to wear. At my gym, there are people there from all walks of life working towards improving their lives. Therefore, no one was thinking about another person! So, what I'm explaining to you is that don't worry when you go to the gym that some health freak is secretly laughing at you. They are too focused on their own physique!
- When was the last time you took a deep breath?
- When was the last time you went on a causal walk?
- Do you keep up with your doctors' appointments?
- Have you just relaxed today?
- Have you told your body you adore it?
- When was the last time you danced naked or in your underwear?

When you ask yourself these questions, pay attention to the messages you receive. This is your body informing you on how to best take care of it. Don't doubt the messages. Be proactive.

The main focus here is to indulge in yourself regularly, not 'every once in a while'. You can do the things described above and so much more regularly. It's like a 'time out' for you to regroup, relax, rejuvenate, and restart!

The Serenity Prayer

God, grant me the serenity to accept the things I cannot change,

Courage to change the things I can,

And the wisdom to know the difference

-Reinhold Niebuhr

Adoring yourself is having the wisdom to know that there has to be a balance in your life of taking care of others, like children or elderly parents, and loving yourself by making time to relax and to rejuvenate. Connect with the Grecian goddess of wisdom, Athena, to gain and maintain your wisdom of what true balance is and what it means to adore yourself!

Athena's Wisdom Decree

Wisdom is within me

I unlock the treasure chest of my wisdom

Wisdom is something I hear, feel, know, and see

With Athena's sword, I remove any falsehoods from my Queen-dom

Wisdom is a great gift and I shall use it in a great way every day

To be of service, to be reasonable, to be fair and just

I evoke my innate goddess wisdom so that it is reflected in everything I do and say

To Be a Goddess of wisdom, all of this is a must

CHAPTER 5
DRESSING AND SPEAKING LIKE A GODDESS

For beautiful eyes, look for the good in others; for beautiful lips, speak only words of kindness; and for poise, walk with the knowledge that you are never alone.
-Audrey Hepburn

Now that you know your symbol, what's your style? What are some of the trends you follow? Maybe you create your own trends or possibly a combo? Either way, the key here is to capitalize on your style. At this point, you also know your dominant colors, main element and to which Goddesses you are closely connected. So, how can you incorporate your color, symbol, element, and Goddess into your world? Well, you can wear an amazing red dress that shows off your awesome tattoo which ignites the fire element within you; thus, connecting you with the goddess Freyja! Furthermore, dressing like a goddess is not limited to what you are wearing. In fact, it extends to everything related such as hair, makeup, and posture!

There are loads of books that will help you to dress by telling you what, and what not, to wear. Therefore, I won't go into detail in that regards. Instead, what I would like to take note of is how the goddesses we have communicated with throughout this book dress, how it relates to us, and how we can incorporate that into our style!

Goddesses like Isis and Quan Yin are usually depicted wearing long flowing divinely looking dresses while wearing a headdress. On the other hand, goddesses like Pele and Freyja are depicted wearing more form fitting, shorter in length, clothing. So, are you more likely to wear clothes that are comfortable and a bit loose, form fitting clothes, or something in between? When you are shopping for an outfit, whether you want to look sexy, casual, or sporty, you can connect with the according goddess and she will lead you to the right outfit! Does what you wear flatter your body type?

A main goal is to display your divinity while creating an air of mystery. Meaning, you want to take care in how you look whether you are the party goddess or the mommy goddess, but give the effect of the 'there is something more about that woman that I would love to discover.'

A woman's dress should be like a barbed-wire fence: serving its purpose without obstructing the view.
-Sophia Loren

How about your makeup? What are the cosmetics you use each day that you cannot imagine leaving the house before applying? For me that would be my concealer, eyeliner, and lipstick. I can have the fresh look and it's quick to apply! Now, think about how you see goddesses' makeup and then think of how that plays a part in her persona.

Don't wear makeup? Not a problem. Some goddesses appear to not wear makeup at all. Think about if you were to wear makeup where would you start? Would you start with a lipstick or gloss or a pencil eyeliner?

Dressing like a goddess is the complete image that you want to portray to the world, which is why I discussed the wardrobe and makeup. But, this also includes the hair, accessories, and posture. Think about it- have you seen a hunched over goddess with unkempt hair looking as if she doesn't care and refuses to help?

Be creative in what you wear! I have seen women with pastel pink colored hair wearing a graphic tee, shorts, fishnet pantyhose in a flower pattern, and boots. She wore accessories and her makeup was simple. Total goddess who found her creative dressing! There are a few goddesses that she could have connected with when she picked her outfit. For example, pink was the main theme for her. Therefore, she could have connected with Quan Yin or Aphrodite.

Dressing like a goddess is a great way to continue to incorporate the goddesses and their energies into our everyday lives. Just like we change our style from day to night, we work with many goddesses at various times. Thus, our energy will emit that energy and it will show through our posture, the colors we choose to wear and so forth.

Watch your thoughts, for they become words. Watch your words, for they become actions. Watch your actions, for they become habits. Watch your habits, for they become character. Watch your character, for it becomes your destiny.

-Gandhi

Words are powerful and we are full of energy. Therefore, the words we say will have an effect. Remember, we always want to be encouraging, speak our truth, and not allow unwarranted negative thinking to sabotage a good friendship. For we are here to help each other improve and reach imaginable and unimaginable new heights! Creating a domino effect of good vibrations!

There are several words that should be in every Goddess' lexicon. The words I listed below are meant to symbolize affirmative thoughts.

- Love/ lovely
- Adore
- Awesome
- Respect
- Understand
- Sexy
- Romantic
- Powerful
- Thank you/ thanks
- Yes
- No
- I AM
- Divine
- Spirit
- Goddess
- God
- Hear
- Support
- Blessings

- ಞ Glorious
- ಞ Relate
- ಞ Amazing
- ಞ What words come to mind?

Now, put the words together to describe yourself or a situation. See below.

- ❖ I love myself
- ❖ No, I'm not available at that time
- ❖ Thanks for the compliment
- ❖ I am powerful
- ❖ I am in a romantic relationship
- ❖ You look lovely
- ❖ I am a Goddess
- ❖ I hear and understand you
- ❖ Spirit is always bestowing upon me blessings
- ❖ I am a Glorious Goddess
- ❖ I can do it!
- ❖ I have an amazing support system

Be plentiful in your compliments and in your self-esteem. A true Goddess will admire and help other Goddesses. Use positive adjectives to describe yourself, others, and various situations to elevate your vibration.

Vent and then let go:

This is one of my mottos I live by and I express on my radio show often. The world isn't always a pleasant place. We experience unpleasant things and we need to talk about those issues! I cannot think of a time when keeping my emotions to myself, in regards to something I felt strangely about, ever being helpful or healthy.

I know 'society' will say and do annoying things like:

- ಅ Just get over it
- ಅ Act like an adult
- ಅ Compare you and your story to someone else's experience that may or may not be relevant

- Change the subject to talk about their selves
- Give you unsolicited advice
- Gossip about you
- Say 'you're complaining'

It is because of reasons like the ones I've listed that cause people to have bottled up emotions! Well, as a goddess, you will say how you feel, tactfully, and then let it go! In other words, go ahead and say how annoyed you were that someone cut you off in traffic or the fact that 'co-worker Bob' was being a jerk today at work. I have learned is that it's not so much what you say as how you say it and who you say it to. So, for example, you can say things like:

- I just don't get why 'co-worker Bob' acted that way at work…
- I was so annoyed today when…
- I get frustrated when…
- …that just doesn't make sense!

So, in a sense, the words are 'negative', but not in a bad manner. It is really acknowledging that there will be good and bad times and both should be expressed. You also want to talk to people you trust because it could be that 'co-worker Bob' was annoying because he unknowingly transferred his emotions onto you as a result of an argument he had with his wife that morning before work; and, has a hard time releasing those emotions. Talking to someone you trust, as opposed to just confronting 'co-worker Bob', creates an atmosphere of 'knowing'; knowing that what you say is not to be repeated to someone else or used for gossip because 'co-worker Bob' could just be experiencing a bad day and is not necessarily a bad guy. Thus, a potential friendship between you and 'co-worker Bob' isn't ruined.

> Speak when you are angry and you will make the best speech you will ever regret.
> -Ambrose Bierce

CHAPTER 6
HELPING OTHER WOMEN TO SEE THE GODDESS IN HERSELF

Carry out random acts of kindness, with no expectation of reward,
safe in the knowledge that one day someone might do the same for you.
-Princess Diana

Helping women to see the goddess within herself will not always be a piece of goddess cake. Therefore, I strongly advise to help those who want help. There are various reasons why a woman would reject her goddess-hood:

- Due to her current religious beliefs, being 'a goddess' is just simply silly or sinful
- She's just not ready to embrace the goddess
- She might think you're on your spiritual 'high horse' and, in spite, chose not to believe you
- It just doesn't make sense to her
- She may have been told she's not pretty and so forth throughout her life; and, therefore, has a difficult time thinking otherwise

No worries here, for everyone has their own path. What is of the utmost importance is that you honor yourself as a goddess. Like attracts like, so when other women are ready to embrace the goddess, they will come to you. It's that kind of 'when the student is ready the teacher will appear' mentality or 'you go where you are needed'. You know what your niche is and you can go forth helping people in that manner.

I must say, there are women I have met whom I immediately saw their beauty! They didn't see it because of various factors. But, it's there! There was a time when I didn't see my beauty! These women that I've met who didn't see their beauty, I constantly encourages them! I didn't overdo the compliments, but I made sure to let the women know that I appreciate their company and they are awesome!

Helping other women see the goddess within their selves creates a ripple effect of greatness. For example:

- You introduce a woman to makeup in order to accentuate her eyes
- She's a bit uncomfortable with the change, but she grows to love the new look
- She gains confidence and starts to update her wardrobe by accessorizing more and so forth
- Her vibration changes and she begins to attract better people and things into her life
- Acknowledging that you have positive intentions, she trusts you more by opening up to you/forming a close friendship
- Her outlook on life changes
- She begins to make bold moves even if she's nervous
- She motivates others to change

The outline above is a demonstration of exactly what happened to me! I was introduced to makeup by my current best friend and then it was, as the saying goes, all she wrote! But, it was a process and it didn't happen right away. I was 'introduced' to makeup, but I perfected how I use the makeup through trial and error. I changed my wardrobe from big sweaters to more form fitting, but still classy, outfits and so forth. My boldest move was switching from glasses to contacts! I've been wearing glasses since I was six years old until I was 25 years old.

Granted, as an adult I wore some very (authentic) stylish Versace or Gucci glasses and I was very satisfied with wearing glasses, but there was a greater plan for me in the making! One day while cleaning my lenses, I broke my glasses! I've been told that I'm 'heavy handed'; however, I just don't realize it and this was the case when I was cleaning my glasses because they broke in half. I was at work when this happened and being extremely near-sighted while trying to type does not make me a very efficient worker. Needless to say, I took it as a sign to try 'something new' and so I did; especially since my aunt and my best friend have been trying to get me to wear contacts for the longest time! Now, I wear colored contacts and I'm very satisfied!!

I have included two photos to demonstrate the kind of transformation I underwent while being encouraged by my best friend and working with the goddesses.

Before: Me beside my best friend, Caroline.   After: Close up of me wearing contacts!

Again, that bold change of transitioning from glasses to contacts was a big deal for me. I was very nervous in the beginning because I wasn't completely comfortable with the change. For a while, I was touching my nose as if to push up my glasses. The compliments I received did help, to a certain extent, me to be more comfortable with the change. If you talk to me, then you will know that I don't seek others to compliment me and so forth; instead, I give myself compliments! But, what I do is ask people whose opinions I value, such as my best friend or my mom, how a dress looks on me or if a particular hair color compliments my complexion.

So, when people complimented me on my contacts, it was helpful mainly because there is a, sometimes huge, difference of how we think we look and how we actually look to the public! Keep in mind that one thing that never changed about me through what I discussed above is that I always loved myself. It was because I loved myself so that I was comfortable with the way I used to look, which prolonged a lot of my transformation. So, just remember to remain open minded because the possibilities are endless and it is okay to feel a little uncomfortable at times when you are doing something new and exciting for your highest good, because what you are really doing is cracking your shell and entering new territory!

What does a woman who is already aware of her goddess-hood gain? Well, that goddess gains the feeling of knowing that she made a friend, helped a woman who wanted help to unlock her goddess nature, and the knowledge that that woman will help another woman who one day will reach her goddess potential. The purpose of helping is not to expect a 'merit' of some sort, for people who are around you on a daily bases will know if you're a person of integrity; if not, then people's intuition will alert them of your true intentions. There is also this not so nice thing called 'gossip', which will spread like wildfire and people will know that you're not helping from the kindness of your heart if you have selfish motives.

There are some really fun ways to help women unleash their inner goddess:
- Go shopping together
- Have a girls night/weekend out
- Take a road trip
- Go to dance classes
- Go out to lunch
- Go out to brunch
- Go to the gym
- Get tattoos
- Just talk
- Share beauty secrets
- Share life experiences
- Do something she always wanted to do

These suggestions are to help develop a relationship with the woman first because if someone just walked up to you and say, 'I see the goddess within you just eager to come out into the world!' Some of you will be thrilled and want to learn more; while others may say, 'Yeah, right! So, I have powers or something?' Honestly, if a woman told me that a few years ago when I was in college, I would have said, 'Really, because I don't feel like a goddess!' And, I would have made some movie reference to the situation. Some things take time. Don't become discouraged if you see potential in a woman who hasn't unleashed her goddess energy, but you have been guided to help her. Just ease into the situation and remember than everyone is on a different path. So, while you're diving into the depths of your goddess energy, another woman is still trying to figure herself out and what she's supposed to do with her life.

Connect with the Welsh goddess of transformation, Cerridwen, to help you as you aid women in their transformation from whatever stage in life they are currently in to diving into her goddess rite!

Cerridwen's Cauldron Decree

I light the fire to ignite change.

I stir the cauldron clockwise to be in the flow of change.

I breathe into the cauldron to give life to the change.

I remain grounded throughout my transformation.

I invite Cerridwen to aid me in this transformation.

CHAPTER 7
MOON CYCLES AND OTHER ASSOCIATIONS OF THE GODDESS

She is the giver of visions… illuminator of the unconscious, revealer of mysterious forces. All tides are hers… tides of death and rebirth… and even the tides of the monthly cycles of women. She is a celestial goddess of dreams... She's a source of physical and spiritual rebirth and illumination... She is the moon--- a powerful spiritual force on our planet and ruler of the dream tides that ebb and flow in the night.

-The Hidden Power Of Dreams

The Goddess chose the moon as her symbol and, as such, the moon has a great impact on our femininity. As we begin to have a better understanding of the moon, and other associations of the Goddess, we will have a better understanding of ourselves. With that being stated, let's dive into the associations of the Goddess and learn how to apply it in our daily lives!

The Moon and Her Phases

In order for the moon to complete her cycle, it takes roughly a month, 29 days, in which time we feel the highs and lows of the energy depending on the particular 'phase' of the cycle. Below, are four major phases I will focus on and what energy we can expect to feel and work with during that phase.

Waxing Crescent Moon

The crescent moon represents strength; and when the moon is waxing, it represents the growth of that strength. During this phase of the moon, it's natural to experience feelings of increased strength and energy as well as a need to formulate ideas and advance in a particular area courageously.

Full Moon

The full moon is the time of heighten energy. It's the peak of your energy. Seeing it completely represents things coming together, being whole. During this phase of the moon, a common feeling is to go out and release the energy, to be active, to celebrate, to do 'something'. This is also a great time to do spiritual work such as goddess rituals and deep meditations. While at the peak of your energy, you are also releasing your energy. So, you may begin to feel like more rest is required right after the full moon.

Waning Crescent Moon

While the crescent moon symbolizes strength, during the time of the waning crescent moon, one can expect to feel a need to release, to de-clutter, and to begin to focus internally. A time of reflection begins.

New/Dark Moon

The phase of the dark moon is a time when the moon cannot be seen. This is a great time for deep reflection, rebirth, and resting. The feeling to start anew begins, making this time a great time for manifesting and meditation as well.

Since our bodies contain a considerable amount of water, it's natural that we are affected by the phases of the moon since the moon affects the ebb and flow of the tides of the oceans and bodies of water. Purchasing an almanac or downloading an app to inform you of the phases of the moon will be very beneficial so you will know which energy to work with during a particular phase in addition to understanding why you are feeling and behaving a certain way!

Full Moon Ritual:

One of the best moon rituals you can do is to draw in the power of the full moon, which is called Drawing Down the Moon. Basically, what you will do is to gaze upon the moon when it's full and imagine that energy gleaming over you as you soak in the energy. In addition, you will call upon the

Goddess and communicate with her your intentions and desires. Below are a few steps to help you make the full moon ritual a great experience. The following ritual can be more detailed. However, I like simplicity when possible!

- Go outside to a safe place where you will not be disturbed and can see the moon. Note: If you are not permitted to go outside or if you cannot see the moon. A picture of moon as well as using your imagination to picture the full moon will suffice.
- Survey the night sky and take several slow deep breaths
- Surround yourself with goddess golden light
- Look at the moon and ask for her wonderful energy to shower over you as you absorb the energy
- Invoke the Goddess and communicate with her.
- When done, thank the moon and the goddess and reflect

The Moon and Menstrual Cycles

- The moon is connected with menstrual blood because it's in relation to being in rhythm with nature and its cycles.
- The suffix of menstrual, -al, means 'of or pertaining to'.
- In Latin, mensis means monthly. However, mensis was also the word for 'moon' in Latin.
- Luna is now the word for moon in Latin.
- Therefore, 'menstrual blood' is blood that is pertaining to the monthly cycle of the moon.
- The moon phases last roughly a week, similar to the time frame of a menstrual cycle.

The monthly menstrual cycles in connection with the moon cycles are, of course, given that we are not experiencing stress or something else that can cause our cycles to become irregular. During our menstrual cycles, we experience many things, such as an increase of our intuition because our senses are intensifying due to that extra surge of energy. As a result, it's not uncommon to have more vivid dreams and visions. This mainly due to the 'connectivity' that happens as we become more in harmony with the rhythms of nature, which include communicating with the goddess and accepting our intuition. A more physical example of being in harmony and connected is when you menstruate the same time as your best friend or another female with whom you are close.

Flowers and the Goddess

I have meditated with each of the thirteen goddesses of this book asking them with which flower do they prefer to be associated. Below is a chart of the flowers, their meaning, and the associated goddess. Deccrate your sacred space by having the actual flowers or pictures of the flowers and focus on tuning into the energy of that flower with the goddess. **Note:** More information in regards to the following flowers can be found in the book *Flower Therapy* by Doreen Virtue and Robert Reeves.

GODDESS	FLOWERS AND THEIR ASSOC.
Isis	Jasmine, Azalea-spirituality and wisdom; Moonflower-balance
Freyja	Baby's Breath-all-purpose; Dianthus-manifests desires such as love, joy, romance, all-purpose
Quan Yin	Lotus-gentle care of balancing of chakras, connecting with divine beings
Brigit	Waratha-courage
Athena	Jasmine-wisdom
Dana	Dianthus-manifests; Sweet Pea-wish granting
Kali	White Rose-cleanses and banishes, transition
Lilith	Black-eyed Susan-increase self-esteem; Mandevilla-empowerment, independence, disbanding attachments
Cerridwen	Hydrangea-transformation
Lakshmi	Clover – abundance; yellow Lily – prosperity
Aphrodite	Cherry blossom – romance; red rose – love
Pele	Banksia – ignite divine flame, passion
Ix Chel	Cactus – healing

Crystals and the Goddess

Just as with the meditation in which I asked the goddesses as to which flowers they prefer to be associated, I asked the same question but in regards to crystals! Below is a chart with the crystals, their meaning, and associated goddess. As you will see, more than one goddess will have the same crystal as a reference. However, the crystals have several properties. Therefore you will see one crystal represent one property for a particular goddess – same crystal represent another property for another goddess.

Note: More information can be found in regards to these crystals in the book *The Encyclopedia of Crystals* by Judy Hall.

GODDESS	CRYSTALS AND THEIR ASSOCIATION
Isis	Pearl – femininity; Moonstone – moon energy
Freyja	Carnelian – courage
Quan Yin	Rose Quartz – compassion
Brigit	Fire Agate – fire element, spiritual strength
Athena`	Diamond – multifaceted wisdom
Dana	Serpentine – good for the Celts, earth element
Kali	Amethyst – connection with spirit, transitions; (blue) Sapphire – transmutes negative energy; third eye
Lilith	Bronzite – deflects negativity, promotes grounding, shrewdness, and noteworthy actions
Cerridwen	Opal – transformation of characteristics, revitalizing
Lakshmi	Yellow Tourmaline – business affairs, personal power
Aphrodite	Moonstone – embodiment of the goddess, Diamond – love, purity
Pele	Fire Opal – awakens your divine fire, promotes sexual passion
Ix Chel	Rainbow Moonstone – spiritual healing, encompasses love and light; malachite – (**note:** malachite is toxic if ingested. Do not ingest or use it to make a gem elixir) deep healing, absorbs negative energy

As a Certified Crystal Healer (CCH), I'm a huge fan of crystals and crystal altars. Below, I describe a way you can make a crystal altar so that you will have a sacred place in which you can draw in the energy of the crystals and the goddess.

- Gather several crystals that you resonates with you
- Get a picture or a statue of a goddess you will be working with to place amongst the crystals
- Put at least one clear quartz on the altar because clear quartz is an amplifier crystal and we want to amplify our energy
- A cloth of the color associated with the goddess or the crystals can be used
- You can set the altar in your room so it won't be disturbed by others
- See picture below of my crystal altar. It's a statue of Quan Yin, a cluster clear quartz, a rose quartz, and a druse amethyst next to my crystal salt lamp.

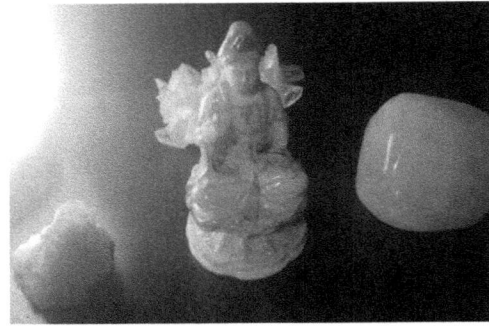

Caring for your crystals:
You can cleanse your crystals several ways. The best way to cleanse your crystals is to place them outside during a full moon. It's ideal to place them where the moonlight can shine directly on the crystals. Another way is to place your crystals besides a clear quartz. Some crystals can be cleansed via the use of water.

The Number 13 and the Goddess

Everything has a vibration, including numbers! As an ANGEL THERAPY PRACTITIONER®, I am thrilled to explain the number 13 in Angel numbers as well as the other meanings behind the 13 and how it relates to the goddess.

In Angel Numbers:

1: Keep your thoughts at a high vibration by maintaining positive thoughts.

3: You are receiving help from ascendant masters such as Quan Yin or other divine spiritual beings.

13: Represents female ascendant masters and goddesses who are helping you in your spiritual path.

   4 (1+3 = 4): The angels are with you and are assisting you.

If we were to put the numbers together, they would mean the following: *keep your thoughts positive and continue to receive help from ascendant masters, such as Quan Yin, and other spiritual beings like goddesses and angels who are assisting you along the way to help you throughout your spiritual path for your highest good.*

Other associations of the number 13:
- Number 1 is a symbol for unity, independence
- Number 3 is a symbol for trinity, self-expression
- Number 13 is a symbol for the goddess, number of moons within a year, of endings and beginnings, love of unity (according to the Kabbalah), the lunar calendar was 13 months, typically a woman have 13 menstrual cycles a year
- Number 4 is a symbol for the 4 elements, manifestations, foundation

A Goddess and Her Divine Flame

A goddess's divine flame is her inner spark of creativity and passion. The more we embrace our intuition, the greater our divine flame. No matter what, the divine flame is always there, in our hearts; sometimes, we just need a reminder that it's there and where to look. Goddess Pele is a goddess of fire, she will aid you in igniting and maintaining your divine flame

Pele's Divine Flame Decree

As I dive into my lower chakras, a volcanic eruption comes forth and my divine flame has ignited

For this is my divine purpose to accept my power, I won't fight it

I shall wield this power for my highest good and use this power passionately

I will never doubt myself or my path, this is the new me

I have a burning desire to complete my goals and, as such, I am trail blazing

A juggernaut I am, a goddess to be, I set myself free

My intentions are always positive and I deflect any negativity

Fire is my element and I am always transforming

Like a Phoenix, I will always rise

And my divine flame, ever powerful, ever the same

A Goddess and Her Nurturing Spirit

All of the goddesses' abilities are based on nurturing; the nurturing of one's spiritual growth, which includes but is not limited to transformation, cycles, and healing. Nurturing comes in many forms. For example, a person's presence or voice can be nurturing by creating a calming effect. The goddess Ix Chel is the goddess of healing and is also known as lady rainbow. We can connect with her to improve our nurturing skills. The rainbow includes all of the colors we can work with for nurturing.

Ix Chel's Nurturing Message

I am the healing goddess and, as such, I lend you the rainbow

Glide across the rainbow and connect with each color, understanding its healing abilities

To be nurturing is to be a compassionate; to be goddess is to be a healer

Connecting with me is to connect with other goddesses; thus we tap into the ultimate healing power of the Universe: perpetual healing

Respect the land, respect the colors, respect the goddesses, respect who you are, respect the power of healing and you will see that you will be healed as well

Allow the rainbow's droplets to fall upon you and be absorbed into your chakras and become the radiant goddess you are

The Charge of The Goddess is a centuries old time honored speech that is normally read at the beginning of a Wiccan (The Wise Craft) ritual by a High Priestess who is speaking on behalf of the Goddess. However, by reading this book in its entirety you are ending an old way of life and beginning a new way of life. Therefore, I thought it appropriate to place The Charge of The Goddess at the end of the book, which is really just the beginning of a new chapter of your life!

In addition, while reciting The Charge of The Goddess, we learned the ancient ways, such as the ideal time to meet with the goddess. Furthermore, The Charge of The Goddess explains that when we celebrate the goddess we are no longer entrapped by the laws of society; and, as a result, she will teach us her esoteric mysteries.

Note: This version of The Charge of The Goddess can be found in the book *Moon Magick* by D.J. Conway

THE CHARGE OF THE GODDESS

Listen to the words of the Great Goddess, who in ancient times was named Artemis, Diana, Astarte, Ishtar, Aphrodite, Venus, Cerridwen, the Morigu, Freyja, the White Lady, and many other names.

Whenever you have need of My aid, assemble in the secret place at least once a month, especially at the Full Moon. Know that My laws and love shall make you free, for no man can prevent your worship of Me in your mind and heart. Listened well and when you come into My presence, and I shall teach you of the mysteries, ancient and powerful. I required no sacrifices or pain of your bodies, for I am Mother of all things, the Creatress who made you out of My love, and the One who endures through all time.

I am the One who is the beauty of the Earth, the green of growing things. I am the white Moon whose light is full among the stars, soft upon the Earth. From Me all things are born, to Me all things, in their season, return. Let My joyous worship be in your hearts, for all acts of love and pleasure are My rituals. You see Me in the love of man and woman, the love of parent and child, the love of humans to all My creations. When you create with your hands, I am there. I blow the breath of life into the seeds you plant, whether of plant or child. Always I stand beside you, whispering soft words of wisdom and guidance.

All seekers of the Mysteries must come to Me, for I am the True Source, the Keeper of the Cauldron. All who seek to know Me, know this. All your seeking and yearning will avail you nothing unless you know the Mystery: for if what you seek you find not within, you will never find it without. For behold, I have been with you from the beginning, and I will gather you to My breast at the end of your earthly existence.

BIBLIOGRAPHY

Auset, Brandi. The Goddess Guide: Exploring the Attributes and Correspondences of the Divine Feminine. Woodbury, MN: Llewellyn Publications, 2009. Print.

Brockway, Laurie Sue., and Laurie Sue. Brockway. The Goddess Pages: A Divine Guide to Finding Love and Happiness. Woodbury, MN: Llewellyn Publications, 2008. Print.

Beak, Sera. The Red Book: A Deliciously Unorthodox Approach to Igniting Your Divine Spark. San Francisco: Jossey-Bass, 2006. Print.

Buckland, Raymond. The Witch Book: The Encyclopedia of Witchcraft, Wicca, and Neo-paganism. Detroit: Visible Ink, 2002. Print.

Buckland, Raymond. Wicca for One: The Path of Solitary Witchcraft. New York: Citadel, 2004. Print.

Conway, D. J. Moon Magick: Myth & Magick, Crafts & Recipes, Rituals & Spells. St. Paul, MN: Llewellyn Publications, 1995. Print.

Cox, Caroline. How to Be Adored: A Girl's Guide to Hollywood Glamour. N.p.: Quadrille, 2012. Print.

Cunningham, Scott. *Cunningham's Encyclopedia of Magical Herbs.* St. Paul, MN: Llewellyn Publications, 1985. Print.

Cunningham, Scott, and David Harrington. Spell Crafts: Creating Magical Objects. St. Paul, MN: Llewellyn Publications, 1993. Print.

Dale, Cyndi, and Cyndi Dale. The Complete Book of Chakra Healing: Activate the Transformative Power of Your Energy Centers. Woodbury, MN: Llewellyn Publications, 2009. Print.

Dugan, Ellen. Practical Protection Magick: Guarding & Reclaiming Your Power. Woodbury, MN: Llewellyn, 2011. Print.

Holland, Eileen. The Wicca Handbook. York Beach, Me.: S. Wieser, 2000. Print.

Judith, Anodea. Eastern Body, Western Mind: Psychology and the Chakra System as a Path to the Self. Berkeley, CA: Celestial Arts, 2004. Print.

Linn, Denise. Secrets & Mysteries: The Glory and Pleasure of Being a Woman. London: Rider, 2002. Print.

Linn, Denise. The Hidden Power of Dreams: The Mysterious World of Dreams Revealed. Carlsbad, CA: Hay House, 2009. Print.

Linn, Denise, and Meadow Linn. *Quest: A Guide for Creating Your Own Vision Quest.* New York: Ballantine, 1998. Print.

Monaghan, Patricia. *The Goddess Path: Myths, Invocations & Rituals.* St. Paul, MN: Llewellyn, 1999. Print.

Nock, Judy Ann. *The Provenance Press Guide to the Wiccan Year: Spells, Rituals, and Holiday Celebrations.* Avon, MA: Provenance, 2007. Print.

RavenWolf, Silver. *To Ride a Silver Broomstick: New Generation Witchcraft.* St. Paul, Minn., U.S.A.: Llewellyn, 1993. Print.

RavenWolf, Silver. *Solitary Witch: The Ultimate Book of Shadows for the New Generation.* St. Paul, MN: Llewellyn Publications, 2003. Print.

RavenWolf, Silver. *To Stir a Magick Cauldron: A Witch's Guide to Casting and Conjuring.* St. Paul, MN, USA: Llewellyn Publications, 1995. Print.

Virtue, Doreen. *Angel Medicine: How to Heal the Body and Mind with the Help of the Angels.* Carlsbad, CA: Hay House, 2004. Print.

Virtue, Doreen. *Archangels 101: How to Connect Closely with Archangels Michael, Raphael, Gabriel, Uriel, and Others for Healing, Protection, and Guidance.* Carlsbad, CA: Hay House, 2010. Print.

Virtue, Doreen. *Archangels & Ascended Masters: A Guide to Working and Healing with Divinities and Deities.* Carlsbad, CA: Hay House, 2003. Print.

Virtue, Doreen. *Goddesses & Angels: Awakening Your Inner High-priestess and "sourceress"* Carlsbad, CA: Hay House, 2005. Print.

Virtue, Doreen, and Robert Reeves. *Flower Therapy.* Carlsbad, CA: Hay House, 2012. Print.

Yogananda, Paramahansa. *Living Fearlessly: Bringing out Your Inner Soul Strength : Selections from the Talks and Writings of Paramahansa Yogananda.* Los Angeles, CA: Self-Realization Fellowship, 2002. Print.

www.ingramcontent.com/pod-product-compliance
Lightning Source LLC
LaVergne TN
LVHW081359060426
835510LV00016B/1900